Parenting Great Girls

Giving Our Daughters
the Courage to
Live Authentic
and Confident Lives

Jeannie Norris

In fondest memory of
Mildred and Woody Jensen,
my loving and wise parents

Contents

PART TWO: Parenting with Perspective

PART THREE: Navigating Unhealthy Landscapes

PART FOUR: Teaching with Purpose

Preface

During my sixteen-year tenure as head of an all-girls boarding and day school, I wrote monthly columns on parenting, on teaching, and most of all, on the challenging issues facing girls as they grow from adolescence toward adulthood. I have collected the essays in this book because of the many times families told me that they put my comments on their refrigerator doors, shared them with relatives, or left them behind in a dentist's waiting room. As a result, I became convinced that the essays had struck a chord not only with parents in my school but also with others who have an interest in the growth and development of adolescent girls.

The essays include short anecdotes about my own growing up in Joplin, Missouri; reflections on ideas I found in news stories or books that I thought would be helpful to parents; my interpretation, as an educator and a parent, of the problems girls face with the onslaught of limiting messages in American media and popular culture; and considerations of the factors that contribute to the most effective learning environment for girls. In the end, though, what I imagine to be the greatest need that I have intuitively sought to fill is the need girls have for patient and wise parents and the need parents have for support and encouragement as they strive to deliver confident and clear responses to their daughters.

These needs, I believe, are rooted both in the deep desire girls have to be authentic and to have agency in their lives and in the aspirations parents have for their daughters to be self-reliant and fulfilled. Our hopes develop in earnest as we see our daughters begin to move beyond the family: I hope she does well in school. I hope others will like her. I hope she has athletic or artistic talent so that she has a way to shine. And along with those hopes come the anxieties: Will she experience success? Will she adjust to the larger world? Will she be accepted? Am I up to the task of supporting my daughter as she begins to navigate the white waters of adolescence?

As an educator in all-girls schools for over thirty years, I have had the time to refine my thinking, in collaboration with other professionals, about what girls need most from the adults in their lives. I have come to understand that they need us to listen to them, to take them seriously, and to support their hopes and dreams. As a result, girls often hear from me that they have important work to do in the world. I encourage them to aspire to have influence, to prepare themselves for their future leadership roles, and to learn how to maintain a stable and authentic center of meaning in their lives. All of this, of course, has to be learned while they are doing algebra, playing soccer, writing English essays, figuring out relationships, and cleaning their rooms. Their work is daunting, to say the least, but girls' position in our culture, as future leaders in every sector and, for many of them, as future parents of the next generation, demands that they develop the self-knowledge that will keep them from being blown off course.

As the faculty in my school developed ways of cultivating confidence and integrity in our students, we began to turn our attention to thinking expansively about what it means to educate girls for lives of purpose. We challenged each girl academically while also teaching her to listen to her inner voice, avoid the influence of limiting messages in the culture, speak her own truth instead of what she perceived others wanted to hear, deal directly with conflict, assume responsibility for solving problems, recover from setbacks, learn from missteps, and formulate life goals. That these initiatives were necessary was undeniable. That we needed to involve parents was also undeniable.

When I was a girl growing up in the fifties and sixties, my parents were surrounded by a community of like-minded adults who supported each other in parenting. These adults shared basic values, and my friends and I heard consistent messages whether we were at home, at church, or at school. Times have changed. Today, parenting can be a lonely endeavor, as families are isolated geographically and beleaguered with demanding schedules that consume every waking moment. In reaching out to parents by sharing the ideas and approaches used here at the school, I also share my philosophy that we are all in this together, all helping girls resist the negative tendencies in the culture, and all in need of working in community to encourage girls' growth and success.

As I reflect on sixteen years of preparing essays for parents, I can see that underlying my thinking is a basic optimism. I believe that if we focus, remember who we are and what we are about as parents, and cultivate the courage of our convictions, we can support our daughters in the most profound ways. It turns out that they want us to be clear and strong, to share what we have learned in life, and to point them in the right direction. They may have formed a habit of not listening and may even be hostile at first to what we have to say, but deep down they need us to fulfill our responsibilities. In short, we don't have to feel helpless as teens teeter and spin. There are things we can do.

The essays that follow describe an array of circumstances that ask for our active participation. Following each essay I have included suggestions for what parents might do. These tips usually take the form of ways we can guide our daughters to think more clearly and deeply about the challenges they confront. We really can stand our ground when they are in meltdown. We really can avoid joining them in their panic and instead coach them in ways to solve problems that will establish lifetime patterns. We really can instill confidence in our daughters and teach them the skills they will need to live lives of purpose and to have influence in what matters most to them. We really can be the competent and courageous parents of our own great girls.

Acknowledgments

I am deeply grateful to the Board of Trustees of Miss Hall's School for giving me permission to publish my essays, which originally appeared in *Columns*, a publication for the parents of Miss Hall's School; to the faculty and staff, who every day create the transformational learning environment I describe in my writing; to the Miss Hall's School students, who delight and inspire me; to Brian Majewski, director of publications at Miss Hall's School, for the nudge and encouragement to move forward with this project; to Elizabeth Debold, whose tutelage over a decade illuminated my understanding of adolescent girls; and to all who suggested that I compile my essays into a collection.

A grateful tribute to designer Amanda Bettis and Kevin Sprague of Studio Two, who create visual magic.

To Marieanne Clark, my editor extraordinaire, whose masterful editing skills, exacting thoroughness, and wise counsel created order out of many small pieces and whose droll sense of humor brightened many long evenings.

To my daughters, Kim and Emily, thank you for helping me find my parenting strength and my voice. Much of what I learned and pass along in this book, you taught me.

To my husband, Peter, thank you. You were my writing teacher, my first gentle reader, my coach and confidant, and without you, none of this would have been possible.

PART ONE:

Finding the Authentic
Adolescent Self

1. Works in Progress
How Girls Grow

I can remember how quickly Mom and I could slide into a shouting match when I was a teen. All would be going along well; perhaps we were standing in the kitchen talking about school or what I wanted for my birthday. Out of nowhere would come the explosion. "We'll need to see," I can hear Mom saying to my suggesting that all my friends come for a slumber party to help me celebrate. "That means it probably won't happen," I spouted back. And we were off and running. Never mind that an hour earlier I had turned down an offer from one of my buddies to sleep over at her house on Saturday night. Miss my family's weekly TV (*Gunsmoke* and *Perry Mason*) and hamburger night? No way. As I look back on those early teen years, I can recall clearly the quick swivel from red-in-the-face anger toward my parents to that feeling of never wanting to leave their side.

This emotional tug-of-war within a girl is a predictable inner sport during the teenage years. Perhaps a useful way to think about this time is to imagine a tunnel that adolescents enter around the age of twelve or thirteen. As parents, we may not notice the gradual movement of our teenage children away from us. But one day we look around and realize that the girl we used to know is gone. Where is the ten-year-old who wanted to hold our hand to cross the street or linger at the dinner table to talk? Every now and then, we catch a glimpse of her—she emerges from the tunnel long enough to wave. Then, she's back inside again for weeks or even months. We are left confused and bewildered.

Communication suffers during this period. How many of us would have to admit that conversations with our adolescent daughters can bring out the worst in us? We have all had the experience of standing toe-to-toe with a fifteen-year-old who *looks* like an adult but acts nothing like one. The dialogue begins; we try to be rational and reasonable. Before we know it, we are tangled up in our own logic. We can't get our point across. We have lost our way and are awash in frustration.

Adolescents are works in progress, and in the past we have attributed adolescent angst and shifting personas to fluctuations in hormone levels. However, research on adolescent brains as reported by the University of California at Los Angeles and the National Institute of Mental Health (NIMH) suggests that the kaleidoscope of behaviors and emotions we observe in adolescents may be related to an expansion of brain cells and neural connections.[1] According to scientists, the frontal lobes, the region of the brain that regulates judgment, emotion, planning, and organization, undergo a huge growth spurt in the teenage years.[2] Yes! we think. Good news! This could explain a lot.

These findings debunk earlier reports, such as the 1997 White House Conference on Early Learning and Childhood Development announcement that most growth in children's brains happens in the first eighteen months of life and that by the time a child is three, brain connections are basically set.[3] I'm certain I wasn't the only parent who wondered if I had cuddled and read to my daughters enough. It's good to learn that the die is not cast before a girl is barely out of diapers.

Discovering that the brain is more malleable during the teenage years than once was thought allows us, parents as well as educators, to create opportunities for adolescents. As a girl moves from puberty to young adulthood, the circuitry in her brain slowly begins to consolidate. The neural connections that a girl uses regularly—to solve calculus problems, read musical notation, or negotiate roommate disagreements—become, as it were, hardwired into her brain. Connections that are not reinforced through use fade away. According to Jay Giedd of NIMH, "Teens have the power to determine their own brain development, to determine which connections survive and which don't."[4]

Those of us who parent and teach adolescent girls also have opportunities in light of these findings. We are better able to understand our young people. For example, here at Miss Hall's School we have observed that girls make quantum leaps in abstract thinking between the ages of fourteen and eighteen. Now we have more insight into why that happens. The data give us a better context in which to try to unravel the mysteries of an adolescent girl's development.

Perhaps the most provocative aspect of this research is what it suggests about the importance of our work with girls in middle to late adolescence. As parents and teachers, we have always understood that we are making deposits into a young bank of intellect that will serve a girl for a lifetime. Understanding more about how a girl's mind develops confirms our commitment to insisting that she take healthy risks, embrace a challenge, and reach for the top. Just as important, we are strengthened in our resolve to nurture her determination, compassion, and integrity, knowing that with these hardwired qualities, a girl will be well prepared for life.

Tips & Tactics

The teenage years are the optimal time for girls to strengthen their brain circuitry for solving problems and making good decisions. The next time your daughter encounters difficulty with these tasks, ask her what she thinks might make the situation better. Listen to her ideas, and respond with another question or comment designed to help her refine her thinking. Can she tell you more about her plan? How does she intend to accomplish it?

2. Authentic Character Building
Personal Authority vs. Conformity

My best friend and I each got a basket purse one spring, the kind with a wooden lid hinged in the middle and a pile of artificial fruit glued to the top. Mine had strawberries; hers, citrus. I started carrying mine right away, but I remember that my friend had to wait until her mother sewed in a liner "so private items couldn't be seen." That bit of propriety went right along with other social rules that were solidly in place in southwest Missouri when I was growing up: Stand when adults enter the room. Don't wear white shoes after Labor Day. Offer your chair to the elderly. Don't use slang or talk too loudly. Convention kept us organized.

Author Tom Wolfe's novel *I Am Charlotte Simmons* is about a young woman, wedged comfortably into the social conventions of Sparta, North Carolina, who slides into a moral abyss when she goes to college and finds that all the rules and social conventions she depended on have disappeared. A high achiever, Charlotte has stacked up a tall pile of prizes, but when her environment fails to provide a moral framework, she falls apart.

In reviewer David Brooks's words, Charlotte is unprepared because "she has never even thought about who she is and how she should actually live, because what she's really addicted to is the admiration she gets when she achieves what others expect her to achieve."[5] Brooks says that Wolfe has "located one of the paradoxes of the age": we carefully educate young people "in all aspects of their lives, except the most important, which is character building."[6] I would say that before we grumble about the lack of character education in academia today, we should ask ourselves why Charlotte doesn't have her own plan for her life.

I am reminded of an anecdote told by the dean of an Ivy League school and recounted in the book *Mother Daughter Revolution: From Betrayal to Power*. In this particular year in the 1990s, "the school had no women Rhodes scholars. . . . The school obviously had young women with excellent grades, athletic talent, and a record of social responsibility. But, when the interviewers asked the candidates what they wanted the Rhodes scholarship for, the girls were floored and had no idea what to say. Wanting [for themselves] had no place in their lives. These were champion 'good' girls, who had done everything right; they were accustomed to doing well," but their accomplishments had always been about meeting others' expectations, not their own.[7]

Before we can expect a young woman to have the courage of her convictions, we need to know that the locus of control for her life is not floating around outside her, as it was for Charlotte. It is now well known that girls quickly pick up on society's cues to be nice at all costs. But when girls become too invested in fitting in and overly sensitive to the needs of others (parents, teachers, peers), they lose control of their lives. They hand over their goals and dreams in return for acceptance. They exchange their personal authority for conformity.

Unless a girl regains control of her life, she will, as Brooks says about Charlotte, be "caught in a maelstrom."[8] Allowing girls to reclaim their essential selves needs to be at the heart of our relationships with our daughters. Character education is not fully effective until girls are back in charge. As parents and educators, we believe that moral courage and integrity are based in self-knowledge. A girl will face the moral challenges that come her way if she values who she is, assumes responsibility for her life, and acts from her own spirit and judgment. This, we say, is being authentic.

Tips & Tactics

Add ten years to your daughter's age to determine a year, pick a day of the week and hour of the day, and ask your daughter where she thinks she will be when that time comes. What will she be doing? The idea is to help her project forward and envision her future. What kind of life does she think she will be living? It does not matter how specific she is in describing her circumstances. What is important is that she develops her ability to reflect on and to practice being able to talk about what has meaning for her.

3. The Challenge to Be Oneself
Advice for Living Well

My idea was to meet in small groups with all the girls here at Miss Hall's School before the end of the term. We called the gatherings *pulse meetings* because I wanted to learn what was on girls' minds. For five weeks leading up to spring break, over plates of freshly baked cookies, we met in groups of eight and talked about life in general.

What is your earliest memory? ("Picking porcupine quills out of my dog's nose.") How old will you be when you have your first child? (Early thirties got the vote.) What would you do if you were the head of school for a day? (Allow students to go out for lunch.) What is the most important lesson to teach children? (Find happiness in small things.) If you had to sum up your life philosophy on a T-shirt in one word, what would yours say? ("Joy" . . . "Happiness" . . . "Faith")

In every group, we eventually got around to discussing the best advice a girl had ever received. Any adult would be impressed with the wisdom imparted by parents, grandparents, and friends. Without question, the Golden Rule was mentioned more than anything else. By the time a girl reaches her teens, we expect her to be able to put herself in another's shoes; nonetheless, it is encouraging that this ancient guide for how to treat others is known and respected by our daughters' generation.

As I listened to other words of advice passed on to girls by their families, I was reminded of how teachers and parents work together to reinforce important messages. What girls remember hearing from Mom or Dad or a favorite aunt is, in most cases, exactly the advice we recommend around here.

What wisdom for living well did girls recall? Don't judge others. Follow your dreams. Choose honesty in all things. Have fun. Don't be greedy. A mistake is a chance to learn. You get back what you put in. Do it right the first time. Life isn't fair. Walk with your head high. Every moment spent unhappy is a moment wasted. Don't cry because it's over; smile because it happened.

There was one area I was interested in exploring, and at least one girl in every group gave me the opening, saying that she had been told to be herself. This gave me the chance to ask, "And how hard is that in today's society?" Trying to catch a glimpse of her true self is one of the hardest jobs facing an adolescent girl. Are there any adults who do not remember floundering around in their own teen years, playing different parts, trying new roles? I couldn't decide who I was going to be when I was fourteen: The quiet scholar, working hard for high grades? The plucky reformer, pointing out every social injustice at my high school? The party girl? (Not being part of the in group, however, made that one tricky.)

From what I heard in the pulse meetings, girls today are much further along in their conscious exploration of self than I could have dreamed of being at their age. For one thing, they understand that being true to yourself is a goal. I'm fairly certain that I didn't even know that when I was teenager. But it is a goal that almost all girls see as "incredibly hard" to achieve. One girl said, "It's a challenge to be yourself when the whole world is trying to get you to conform." Another student added, "Sometimes, just to be popular, you end up creating something that isn't you." Still another student's remark confirms the maturity of girls' thinking today: "The important thing is not to change for someone else." How many years did it take my generation to figure that out?

Eventually the discussions about being yourself came around to a conversation about voice. "Are you willing to risk membership," I asked, "by speaking your mind?" Girls knew exactly what I was talking about.

One girl said that once she decided not to belong to the popular group at her middle school, she could say anything she wanted. Another student, who mentioned that she speaks out much more than she did in her coed school, said, "When I give my opinions, I can tell who my real friends are." Another student noted that she sees the issue as not about what you lose by speaking up, but about what others gain from hearing your voice.

Throughout these conversations, I was reminded of David Elkind's *All Grown Up and No Place to Go: Teenagers in Crisis*. He talks about how we create psychological stress for ourselves when we "satisfy a social demand at the expense of a personal need, or vice versa."[9] The major task in managing that stress, he adds, is to "find ways to balance and coordinate the demands that come from within with those that come from without."[10] Much of the work of the adolescent years, as my conversations with the students suggest, is about a girl figuring out how best to balance her needs with the needs of those around her. We support her in doing that work when we guide her to develop "a healthy sense of self and identity," that is, "a whole set of attitudes, values, and habits that can serve both self and society."[11] The self-esteem that emerges in a young person as a result, says Elkind, can be defined as "liking and respecting oneself and being liked and respected by others."[12] What parent does not want this for a daughter?

We ended every meeting with the same exercise: each girl had to tell one other girl something about her that she admired. Girls do this with grace and eloquence. Each girl left my office feeling affirmed for something she is or does well. Part of developing a healthy sense of self is receiving confirmation from others.

Tips & Tactics

Suggest to your daughter that she and her friends design T-shirts with their life mottos on them. To get started, you might ask them to think of the best advice they ever received or to consider what advice they would give a younger girl.

•••

Ask your daughter to describe a time she took a stand for what was right. How did that make her feel? Ask her where she got the courage to do what she did.

• • •

Talk with your daughter about how she balances her needs with those of others. Ask her if she can remember a time when she felt she had to respect herself and let that priority guide her. Does she think others respected her for it?

4. To Tell the Truth
Equipping Girls for Self-Discovery

A friend who heads another school for girls uses the metaphor of packing a book bag when she welcomes back faculty and staff every fall. "What will you put in your book bag for this year?" she asks. Likewise, I have been thinking about what girls who arrive on campus each fall need in their book bags. In addition to a laptop, earphones, a calculator, and sweatpants, what does an adolescent girl need for a successful year?

Here at Miss Hall's School, we talk with girls about the important work of discovering oneself. "Who are you?" we ask. "Who is it that looks back at you when you look in the mirror? Whose song do you sing? Who will you become?"

When you think back to when you were fourteen or fifteen, do you remember your struggle to discover who you were? You appeared to be one person at home, another with your friends. Then, if someone of the opposite sex walked into the room, you changed completely. It is partly the memory of this chameleon existence that makes it easy for most of us to agree that we have no interest in repeating our teenage years, even if we could. There is something unsettling about not knowing where the center is, of feeling that any one of several personalities could pop out at any moment.

In addition to figuring out algebra and the past perfect tense of French verbs, adolescent girls must also figure out who they are. I am reminded of that old television game show *To Tell the Truth*. Who is the real girl who stands up when her name is called? Who is the real self, that self that is bigger than the thinned-down, air-brushed image so prevalent in movies and fashion magazines? Our job as parents and teachers is to acknowledge that discovering who she is must be a critical part of every girl's secondary education curriculum. In addition to teaching her algebra and French, we must make certain that we help equip her for the task of self-discovery.

What goes into the book bag to help girls with this work of self-discovery? Basically, a generous slice of time, lots of caring adults, and a safe, comfortable space. Girls need time to try on different roles for size and fit. At Miss Hall's School, the change we see in a student from the opening day of her first year to the day she steps forward to receive her diploma is staggering. In the interim, she has traveled down many paths, recast herself many times, and announced to the world a certain direction, only to change her mind by dinnertime. This exploration cannot be rushed. Young lives cannot be so crowded and pressured to meet the demands of adults that there is no time or energy left for the job of growing up.

Adults who work with girls must have patience for the journey and reverence for the process. It is our job to see through the masks and costumes to the truth and the promise in each girl. We hold the mirror. Looking beyond the awkwardness and false starts, we catch a glimpse of a physicist, a painter, or a president. It is all about not letting a girl settle for what lies only within the limits of her viewing screen.

With so many changes in her life, the last thing an adolescent girl needs is shifting sand beneath her feet. She must be able to depend on a stable environment; structures and expectations; and adults who respond to her in consistent, supportive, and predictable ways as she elbows her way through the last chapter of childhood and prepares for college and life. It is time, caring adults, and a safe setting that are most needed in every girl's book bag when she arrives at her school on opening day. That is our gift to our daughters.

Tips & Tactics

Make it your goal to point out to your daughter something you recently noticed about her that is admirable. Perhaps she helped negotiate a peaceful resolution to a conflict. Maybe she took charge of a project, and everyone reached the goal. She may have offered friendship to a girl who had been left out, or she may have refrained from engaging in gossip. Take time to tell your daughter what you observed and to praise the maturity of her actions.

•••

Ask your daughter if she can describe a time when she influenced the outcome of a situation. Did she speak up at the critical moment? Did she have a creative solution to a problem?

5. A Life in Reflection
Teaching Girls to Be Thoughtful Life Practitioners

I was sixteen years old with a new driver's license in my wallet when Dad handed me the car keys and said, "Let's go to the store. You drive." Without incident we arrived at Thriftway, and I nosed the car into a parking space. Fifteen minutes later, shopping finished, I backed the car out, put it in drive, turned the steering wheel as far as it would go to the right, and stepped on the gas. Whiz! We sped forward, missing by a hair the back fender of the car that had been parked next to us. "What were you thinking?" my dad yelled. Incredulous, I barked back, "I turned the wheel as far as it would go!" "Well, it's only sheer luck that kept you from hitting that guy!" was Dad's exasperated retort.

The fact is, I hadn't thought about anything other than what I had been taught in Drivers Ed: turn the wheel and drive forward. The idea that I might need to assess the radius of the turn and take several stabs at it before I would clear the car ahead never entered my mind.

Social scientist Donald Schön wrote extensively on the importance of combining learning by doing with the traditional school-based acquisition of facts and concepts. His work focused on the professions, the sector to which society has turned over the past century to help make sense of what Schön called the "explosion of the 'knowledge industry.'"[13]

Schön noted that increasingly "both professional and layman have suffered through public events which have undermined belief in the competence of expertise and brought the legitimacy of the professions into serious question."[14] Although Schön was writing about the two decades following 1963, we have no problem, particularly in the wake of September 11 and a few stock-market meltdowns, in questioning the competency of those who are supposed to be in charge and in believing that somehow, somewhere, someone is just not doing the job.

The reason things break down, according to Schön, is that professional schools teach students theories and how to apply those theories to solve well-known problems without educating these students in how to handle the unexpected, the everyday servings of complexity and ambiguity that life dishes up.[15] His theory is that real-world problems do not fall into "well-formed structures."[16] "Indeed," he says, "they tend not to present themselves as problems at all but as messy, indeterminate situations."[17] There are, of course, professionals who are extremely competent, but that is not, Schön says, because they have more professional knowledge, but because they possess a "professional artistry" that allows them to work effectively in "unique, uncertain, and conflicted situations of practice."[18]

At the heart of this professional artistry is Schön's theory of reflection-in-action. Basically, what he says is that when we are taken by surprise and faced with uncertainty, instability, and conflicting values, we need to reflect on what we are doing as we are doing it and thus "reshape what we are doing as we are doing it."[19]

An adolescent girl is taken by surprise almost every day. She rarely wakes up as the same person two days in a row. Uncertainty surrounds her, and she is thrown headlong into the arena of competing interests and ethical dilemmas. Our job as parents and as educators, therefore, is to coach girls in the artistry of life.

Every time we ask girls to question their assumptions, to put themselves in someone else's shoes, to take a healthy risk, to set priorities, to restate a problem, to deal with unintended consequences, or to manage the crucible moments involving discipline and disappointments, we are teaching them to be reflective life practitioners. This kind of "turn[ing] thought back on action" or "framing the problem," as Schön refers to it, happens for a girl hundreds of times each week, either in the classroom, on the playing field, or in her room at the end of the day.[20]

As important as these approaches are, the greatest benefit to girls as they attempt to live reflective lives is to be in the presence of reflective teachers and parents. The surprises that confront *us* as we teach and parent girls often require us to reset the problems that emerge. Just as Schön asks the practitioner to take seriously the uniqueness of unexpected situations and to find new meanings, we must acknowledge that in raising competent girls, we will face unexpected events because each girl standing before us is a unique person. We can have hopes and dreams for her future. But when something happens that challenges our preconception of who she is or what her future will be like, we need to be willing to stop, to reflect, and to reexamine our expectations.

As reflective adults, we need to adopt a coaching style when teaching or parenting girls. We can tell, but we also must listen. We can know that a girl has much to learn, but we cannot overload her with information. We can acknowledge that a girl's inability to understand often has more to do with our deficiencies than with hers. We can respond in a way that keeps inquiry moving. We can invite a dialogue about misunderstandings. Finally, we can know that a girl's life can only be lived by her.[21]

Tips & Tactics

The next time your daughter achieves a goal (a good grade or a winning basket, for example), ask her to tell you how she accomplished that goal. Was it practice? Did she set a personal goal? If so, what are the steps she followed once she made her commitment? Listen for any sign that she is dismissing her contribution. For example, she might attribute her success to luck or to an easy test. If she starts down that road, refocus her on what she brought to the work of being successful.

• • •

Ask your daughter to write down her five greatest strengths. Review the list with her. How many strengths have to do with caring for others? We want our daughters to be compassionate and sensitive to others' needs, but those qualities should appear alongside other personal qualities that reflect courage; honesty; and intellectual, artistic, or athletic attributes.

6. Taking the Lead
Helping Girls Own Their Lives

I was secretary of the Solo and Ensemble Club at my large public high school in the Midwest. (Girls were always secretaries, not presidents.) The meetings were actually minirecitals performed by all of us young classical musicians. One had to be approved for membership, something I guess we did to ensure a certain standard of performance. At one point I became aware that an accordion player wanted to join the group and that most of the club members were opposed. It wasn't the individual they objected to; accordion music was just too lowbrow.

Personally, I didn't care for accordion music (although Lawrence Welk was a favorite of my parents). Nonetheless, my adolescent moral sensibilities had been awakened, and I decided to speak out against what I perceived to be a gross injustice to the student involved. Seeking the advice of my parents and other mentors, I wrote a speech that I practiced delivering in front of a mirror to be certain my presentation would be laced with plenty of conviction. The day came for me to make my case. Feeling simultaneously sweaty and cold as well as slightly queasy, I walked to the front of the classroom. With knees knocking, I advocated for the boy to be approved, saying that we needed to be exposed to all kinds of music at our age.

Something about the culture of that specific school allowed me to take a risk and be who I needed to be. It wasn't easy. In fact, it was harrowing. However, the experience of taking a controversial stand made a lasting impression and was for me, as it is for all young people, a necessary step in a life-long journey toward self-awareness and fulfillment.

Unfortunately, the opportunity for self-assertion is not universally or easily available in our society. We have created a culture in which the pressure for girls and young women to conform and fit in is often immense. In 2003, Duke University launched the Women's Initiative, a university-wide research project to assess the status of women in all aspects of the institution. In one of her updates on this project, then Duke president Nannerl O. Keohane described undergraduate life, noting that "suffocatingly complex codes tell college women what to wear, how to act, what to eat and drink, which weight machine is for guys and which for girls, how many hours they are 'allowed' to study, whom they may have sex with, how they should treat their younger peers. I am concerned about their high level of conformity to harsh norms and the resultant problems of self-esteem."[22]

More recently, Princeton University undertook a study of women's leadership on its campus and found that since the year 2000 there has been a decrease in female presence in the most visible leadership roles and other prominent positions.[23] Comparative data from other institutions indicate, furthermore, that Princeton is not alone in seeing this downturn and that the patterns "are common on other campuses."[24]

A number of themes emerged during the study, and they suggest that the decline in women's involvement in higher echelon roles is related to "differences—subtle but real—between the ways most Princeton female undergraduates and most male undergraduates approach their college years."[25] One of these differences is that "women, more than men, are pressured to behave in certain socially acceptable ways."[26] Women are "supposed to be smart . . . and also 'pretty, sexy, thin, nice, and friendly,' as one undergraduate reported."[27] Women, however, are not to be "so . . . smart as to be threatening to men."[28]

What is wrong when high-achieving young women (the profile of students admitted to Duke and Princeton) are unable to set their own standards and norms? The basic issues have to do with the individual: the level of confidence a young woman has in speaking out, the value she places on her own life experiences and lived knowledge, and the degree to which she is able to assert her personal authority as a result of her confidence in knowing what she knows.

As educators, we tackle these issues every day at Miss Hall's School. Every time we ask a girl for her opinion or point out the uniqueness of her insights, we confirm the value of her ideas. Each time we insist that a girl take the lead in working through difficulty, we communicate our confidence in her ability to solve problems. When we invite a girl to question the status quo, we raise her awareness of her own potential for making change in the world.

The result of supporting a girl's growth in this way is that she learns to keep the locus of control for her life within her. She comes to understand that her reliable guides are her own aspirations for how she will have influence in the world and not the culturally dictated stereotypes that others promote as models. Most importantly, she discovers that asserting herself on behalf of her own authentic desires is the only way to make her dreams come true.

Tips & Tactics

Before the next marking period rolls around at your daughter's school, suggest to her that you are interested in her assessment of how things are going. Ask her to include in her self-report card all her subjects in school, her extracurricular activities, other activities in her life, friendships, and her health and wellness. For each item, suggest she respond to the following:

- Overall, how am I doing in this area?

- What am I very pleased with?

- What could be going better in this area?

- What might be a first step to help me improve in this area?

7. Talking the Talk
Emerging Voices of Confident Girls

Nancy, my best friend until junior high, lived across the alley from me. As the saying goes, we were attached at the hip and thus spent all our unscheduled time together. Back when I was a girl, this was any time that we weren't in school or church. As close as we were, however, I can remember more than one screaming match, disagreements usually prompted by decisions of such epic import as whether this week's arrangement for the playhouse would be an office or a New York City apartment. As I grew older and moved on to junior-high and high-school friends, I remember few, if any, spats. Fitting in and getting along were absolute priorities, and that required me to tone down my behavior.

I grew up in a time when young people were seen and not heard. Helping me find my voice was on no one's must-do list. Times have changed, and we are committed to encouraging girls to speak their minds. Nonetheless, we are aware that from a girl's perspective, being compliant still brings great rewards. Authors Jill McLean Taylor, Carol Gilligan, and Amy Sullivan write in *Between Voice and Silence: Women and Girls, Race and Relationships*, "Girls who by virtue of their class position, their cultural status, or their educational privilege have been led to believe that people are interested in who they are and what they have to say, worry about jeopardizing these relationships by revealing what seem like unacceptable parts of themselves. They will often modulate their voices to blend in. In short, girls . . . will often be persuaded . . . to give up their questions in order not to jeopardize their chances."[29]

Furthermore, as a culture we're still not sure how assertiveness fits in with femininity. Just how outspoken can one be and still have a date for Saturday night? Selflessness is also a feminine ideal in our society. Can one be selfless *and* ambitious? A girl might wonder, can I advocate for myself and also be a good friend to others?

Helping each adolescent girl work through these dilemmas and become comfortable with her authentic voice is central to our mission at Miss Hall's School. This work, however, requires that educators and parents alike be undaunted when that strong voice erupts and that we respond with thoughtful coaching. Although girls may have learned to modulate their voices to blend in, they need us to help them learn to modulate their voices to speak out and be heard.

Most girls who are discovering how to challenge, to contest, and to debate are not yet ready to do so with the level of refinement that characterizes high diplomacy. The focus for girls, understandably, is on how to hurdle the emotional risks involved with setting oneself apart. As they are summoning the courage to speak up, their words can pop out in blunt, accusatory, or insensitive ways. What we as a faculty understand is that these utterances require the same response as any other faulty answer in class. We correct the response but support a girl fully in finding a better one. Most importantly, we keep our own emotions under control. Just as we remain emotionally neutral when a girl miscalculates in solving for x, we try not to take it personally when she miscalculates in being assertive. Although a girl may sound like an adult when she is emoting, it is the mark of a great teacher to recall that this girl is still a fifteen-year-old student.

This approach is not business as usual. Unlike boys, girls traditionally are seen as being ideal students because they are easier to control. Peggy Orenstein warns in *Schoolgirls: Young Women, Self-Esteem, and the Confidence Gap* that the "praise girls earn for their exemplary passivity discourages them from experimenting with the more active, risk-taking learning styles that would serve them better in the long run."[30]

Preparing girls for their future is our mission as parents and as educators, and we want girls to become comfortable with the sound of their own voices, in controversy as well as in agreement. Nuanced expression that is respectful and understanding as well as honest and effective takes practice to achieve. We know that we must model that language every day. Over time, in an environment that values authenticity in girls and has the collective wisdom and patience to encourage and nurture it, girls prepare fully for lives of great purpose.

Tips & Tactics

Ask your daughter whether or not she feels comfortable speaking out in her classes. You may learn from her that it is the boys who speak most often. If your daughter is in elementary or middle school, consider speaking with her teacher about the gender dynamics of classroom discussions. If your daughter is in high school, ask her what she thinks would make it possible to speak out more. Regardless of how well girls perform as measured by grades, they learn that their opinions aren't valued if they are silent in class.

• • •

The next time your daughter becomes confrontational, try to remember the following:

- Don't take it personally.
- Be calm but firm in reminding her that respect for others is nonnegotiable.
- Tell her you want to hear what she has to say as soon as she can say it calmly.

8. Can We Talk?
Group Conversation and Problem Solving

Feeling unusually glum, even for a mid-February afternoon, I sat down at the lunch table with a group of students. "I've just received a letter from an acquaintance with some disappointing news," I said in answer to one girl's inquiry about my day. "Want to talk about it?" she quickly responded. How comfortable that offer felt! This is a female thing, I thought. Got a problem? Talking will make it better.

Talking and listening are healing, says Mary Pipher in her book *The Shelter of Each Other: Rebuilding Our Families*. "The Native Americans of the Southwest have talking circles," she writes, "in which everyone explains her point of view about situations or events."[31] It's not so different here at Miss Hall's School. Within the structure of a confidential and secure setting, girls gather on a regular basis to talk about such things as body image, stress management, wellness, friendships, and conflict resolution.

As a way to deal with the world, talking isn't new. When I was the age of these girls, I also talked my way through the issues that confound adolescent girls. However, that was back in the sixties. No one was forming a formal discussion group where I went to school. Girls got together and sorted things out on their own. We kept our talks hidden away, after hours and behind the scenes.

Things have changed since then. Our daughters have grown up in a world that is saturated with talk and influenced by the idea of talk as therapy. Every sensitive topic known to humankind is discussed on afternoon TV talk shows, and advice flows freely. Dealing with our personal problems in a context of group conversation and support is definitely in vogue. Indeed, the talk of our girls often contains the language of self-help psychology. Today's adolescent girls understand self-esteem. They know that if they are feeling bad, it is possible to deal with that feeling. Seeing a counselor is commonplace, and for many families a counselor has become standard equipment, much like the pediatrician or the drycleaner. In fact, we are all a lot more familiar and comfortable with the notion that our psyches need care and attention just as our physical bodies do, and we are better equipped to discuss the issues that challenge us.

I am glad that this is the climate for my work as head of an all-girls school. As I travel around and meet with alumnae, I am aware that today's adolescent girls are far more empowered to speak up and talk about what bothers them than their counterparts from other generations. An alumna from the class of 1934 once told me that she and her classmates were never allowed to make any of their own decisions; all decisions concerning her were made by her parents or by the head of school, Mira Hall. Some alumnae from the fifties and sixties remind me that things had not changed much by the time they arrived at Miss Hall's School. It was rare that they were asked their opinions or that there was an invitation for them to talk through their problems.

That is not the way we are rearing girls today. We want them to grapple with the complexities of the world, to weigh their options, to talk their way through to good decisions. There is a danger, however, in going overboard on me-centered talk. Focus on self must be balanced with focus on others. But the bottom line is that girls' natural inclination to solve problems in relationships must be validated and supported at school and at home. It is a much healthier way to grow up.

Tips & Tactics

Watch for signs that your daughter is giving you the answers she thinks you are looking for. For example, she may say that everything is fine when you can see that she is feeling the opposite of fine. Even if she is not ready to discuss what is troubling her, let her know you are available if she would like to run some ideas by you. You may also want to mention that talking things through often helps you know whether or not you're on the right track. Give her examples of people who have helped you sort through confusing issues to arrive at a decision.

9. Essential Rebellion
Challenges and Healthy Risks

I don't know what the problem was. Maybe Dad had said no to something I wanted or maybe he was giving me a tune-up talk. What I do remember is that I didn't like it, and before I knew what was happening, I stuck out my tongue. It was the wrong move, and I knew it right away. Clear that things were about to go from bad to worse, I did what many of us do when we experience fear—I fled. With a quick turn, I ran out the side door and up the street as quickly as my ten-year-old legs would carry me. Dad was in hot pursuit, and when it occurred to me that I couldn't outrun him, I stopped. I was in serious trouble, but that rebellious streak had gotten the better of me. As I recall, I had plenty of opportunity in the time-out chair to reflect on my behavior.

My choice to rebel in such an unpleasant manner certainly needed the response it got, but when I was growing up there was little tolerance for any kind of dissent or dispute. Children truly were to be seen and not heard. Even throughout my teen years, the encouragement we now give girls to assert their opinions, to challenge, and to disagree was rarely offered. Helping an adolescent find confidence, even through awkward assertions of opinion, was typically not part of the parenting or teaching pedagogy those many years ago.

Harvard University president Drew Gilpin Faust, a contemporary of mine, recalled in a *New York Times* article that she grew up "in a world where social arrangements were taken for granted and assumed to be timeless. A child's obligation was to learn these usages, not to question them."[32] Faust also described the confrontations she had with her mother about how to interpret being feminine. Certainly, as teen girls in the sixties, Faust and most of the women of our generation struggled to lock in a clear picture of what it meant to be a woman as the cultural lens was continually spun out of focus in those turbulent years.

Over time, many of our generation did develop comfort with personal authority, but the timing for that development varied depending on life experiences. Faust attended both an all-girls boarding school and Bryn Mawr College, one of the prestigious Seven Sisters women's colleges. There she learned what girls here at Miss Hall's School learn today, that having influence and making change is a way of life. In her case, she successfully challenged the college's rules on curfew and organized a campaign to extend out-of-room time, just as girls here challenged our cell phone policy and formulated ways to reevaluate that policy.[33]

Women without the advantage of a single-sex education may recall a professional colleague who intervened to confirm and validate their opinions. Many of us also have undertaken a baptism-by-fire assertiveness course when we were faced with managing our own rebellious teenage children. In whatever circuitous route our individual journey has taken, however, most of us now in our fifth and sixth decades have arrived in that place where we can comfortably be who we need to be.

What struck me in the *New York Times* article, however, was Faust's comment about being surprised "by how my life turned out."[34] In other words, she said, "I've always done more than I ever thought I would."[35] There are many women of our generation who would agree, as I would, that the step-by-step realization of our ambitions has often included an element of surprise. In contrast, assumptions regarding the value of their contributions are anchored firmly in today's Miss Hall's School students. Our young women now expect that they will set goals and achieve them because they believe that they matter and that their contributions are essential.

As teachers and parents, we are ambitious for our students and daughters and encourage them every day to take the kind of healthy risks that advance their knowledge and build courage. Think of the head start they have because we cheer on their respectful rebellion! When one of our girls one day assumes the presidency of a major university or even a country, she will be grateful for the opportunity, but she won't be surprised.

Tips & Tactics

Over dinner or at another time when there are family discussions under way, whether about current events or about a destination for the family vacation, ask your daughter for her opinion. (Focusing on current events in particular gives her the opportunity to engage with large complex issues outside the constraints of a school setting.) Look for moments when you can confirm the value of her ideas and opinions: "Interesting insight. I would never have thought of that."

10. When No One Is Watching
Ethical Decision Making in the Twenty-First Century

Y ou couldn't get away with naughtiness if you were a child growing up in Joplin, Missouri, in the fifties and sixties. Joplin was a fishbowl. Everyone knew what everyone else was doing, and kids were the most carefully scrutinized. Everywhere I hung out, people knew who I was and to which parents I belonged. At the Dairy Queen, Buford's Market, or the Fox Theater on Main Street—if I had made a misstep anywhere, my mom and dad would have known about it within the hour. As far as school was concerned, my father always said, "If you get in trouble, there'll be more trouble when you get home." My parents and teachers were in cahoots, and they weren't having any mischief.

Thinking back, I realize that there were fewer ways to misstep then than now. A small town naturally had fewer temptations, and young people in general did not have as much access to adult distractions as kids have today. The Internet, which is at the center of so many behavioral dilemmas, didn't exist.

Like every other school, Miss Hall's School spends a significant amount of time helping girls navigate the rough ethical waters stirred up by technology. We have Internet usage rules, but when so much is accessible with just a click of the mouse, it is nearly impossible for many teenagers to resist temptation. Addressing the students after disciplinary incidents involving infractions of our Internet rules, I find myself saying over and over, "Just because you can, doesn't mean you should." I'm forthright with girls in telling them that there are more ways for them to outsmart us and our systems than there are safeguards for us to use. In other words, what the situation requires is individual restraint and commitment to doing what is right, even when no one is watching.

What makes teaching basic values more difficult these days is adolescents' broad awareness of wrongdoing in our society's highest offices. As girls worry about properly citing the intellectual property of others, prominent historians, researchers, and college presidents are called on the carpet for quoting sources without attribution. While we mete out consequences for girls who disregard our rules for respecting personal property, CEOs make decisions that devalue the retirement accounts of thousands of innocent people.

Helping adolescents develop a moral identity has surely been a challenge throughout history. At ages fourteen through eighteen, girls have barely entered the stage of growth in which empathy becomes a possibility. Most girls at this stage are preoccupied with their newly discovered powers and problems and thus must be coached into recognizing that impulses need to be tempered, both for the greater good and for their own good. Educators believe that there is no more noble work than helping young people develop their personal virtues, what authors Kevin Ryan and Karen E. Bohlin call the "habits of the head, heart, and hand that enable us to know the good, love the good, and do the good."[36] As those of us over thirty know, this is a lifelong endeavor.

A few years ago, I met with each girl in the school and asked what advice had the most meaning in her life. The Golden Rule was number one. Moms and dads, grandparents, and other family members had passed along the ancient do-unto-others wisdom, and girls had embraced it. This litmus test of ethical decisions is important for all of us, particularly our teenagers. Philosopher and ethicist Carol Tauer offers other measurements that allow us to explain abstract ideals in a way that adolescents and adults can easily understand. According to Tauer, *role reversal* asks a girl if she would be willing to exchange places with the person who is most disadvantaged by her decision.[37] *Universal consequences* suggests that she consider what the consequences would be if everyone made the decision she has made.[38] *Publicity* encourages the girl to ponder how comfortable she would be in having the action she has chosen announced on CNN.[39]

It is important for us as parents and educators to tell girls how difficult it is for all of us, adults and adolescents alike, to pursue a life of virtue. At the same time, it is our modeling of virtuous behaviors that has the most lasting influence on our daughters and students. In this age when the lines between children and adults are so blurred, it is crucial that we not shrink back from guiding those who look to us for moral direction. We each must accept the role of responsible adult and be willing to tell girls what they need to know, not just what they want to hear.

Tips & Tactics

Look for opportunities to share your thoughts about ethical decision making with your daughter. When she is stumped and facing an ethical dilemma, suggest that she ask herself the following questions:

- Would I want to see what I am about to do described in the local newspaper or on the Internet tomorrow?

- Would I want my grandmother, aunt, or other relative to know what I am about to do?

- Would I want to live in a school (or in the world or in a group) where everyone does what I am about to do?

11. The Patience Fuse
Encouraging Self-Control

It was during the summer after my ninth-grade year that Mom, Dad, my brother, and I loaded up the turquoise Plymouth for our vacation. We were driving from Joplin to California, taking the southern route through the deserts of Arizona and Nevada. Air conditioning? Not in our car. The plan was that we would wet down Mom's tea towels and put them on our heads as we headed into desert areas. Sure enough, the wind from the car window blew through the towels and kept us cool until the towels dried out, which they did, quickly. We endured the heat until the next gas station, where we redampened the towels. We had tap water in our gallon thermos, of course, but that was only for drinking. Needless to say, at fourteen I was impatient and frustrated with the whole arrangement, particularly with the result of a wet towel on my hair.

I didn't handle frustration well back then, and neither do most teens today. In fact, girls growing up in our culture of immediate gratification have every reason to develop a much shorter patience fuse than girls growing up when I was a teen. As a society, we want everything instantly, from messages and movies to weather and weight loss. Girls have grown used to a rapid-results lifestyle. Furthermore, as parents we have stumbled over ourselves in our rush to accommodate our children's requests. The standard responses of "we'll see" or "we'll talk about it later" uttered by my parents are, I suspect, heard far less often now.

Overlay this mouse-click time frame on a stage of development that is historically known as an impatient age, and our work is cut out for us. As parents and as educators, we want girls to adopt a thoughtful approach to decision making and to managing their lives. However, it is well documented that there are biological as well as cultural causes for teens' irritation with process and adult intervention when they come in the form of imposed safeguards and restrictions. The prefrontal cortex, the part of the brain that governs reasoning, planning ahead, and managing impulses, develops much later than once thought—not until the midtwenties.[40] Until that development takes place, it's difficult for many teens to understand and accept our more measured slant on the world.

David Walsh, author of *Why Do They Act That Way? A Survival Guide to the Adolescent Brain for You and Your Teen,* is quoted in an ABC news release as saying, "If we were to compare the teenage brain to an automobile, it's as if the gas pedal is to the floor, and there are no brakes."[41] However, Dr. Grazyna Kochanska, a professor at the University of Iowa, states in the same news release that the environment we provide for growing children can make a difference. The author of a longitudinal study on how self-control can be encouraged in young people, Dr. Kochanska says that when they can develop in a setting that is "supportive . . . well-organized, and predictable," they will learn to delay gratification and become more patient.[42]

Supportive, well organized, and predictable describe the environment here at Miss Hall's School. I often discuss girls' needs for secure boundaries and for adults who are confident and unflappable when it comes to adolescent drama. An enlightened firmness from parents and from teachers lets girls feel safe while they are figuring out who they are.

As parents and as educators, we need to go one step further. Knowing that girls will be able to tolerate frustration better when they feel in control of their lives, we engage with them in ways that require them to search for deeper meaning, not only in the academic curriculum, but also in the course of study that is about building greater confidence and self-reliance. Whether in the classroom or in conversations about the myriad issues on girls' minds, we question more than we answer. By asking a girl to clarify, elaborate, describe alternatives, examine assumptions, predict outcomes, evaluate options, identify resources, and create a plan for moving forward, we are giving her the tools to understand a complex world and are confirming our belief in her ability to think for herself. We are making it possible *for her* to form a sturdy internal identity to take with her when she leaves the security of home and school.

Remember the connect-the-dot books we had as kids? When we drew lines between numbers in the right order, we saw the pictures. This is what teens must do. As parents and as teachers, we will provide the matrix for growth, but our job is not to rush to the rescue when girls are trying to connect the dots. When girls call home or walk through the door in total frustration, wise parents will be ready to engage, not with answers, but with queries. Working from questions written out in advance if necessary, moms and dads can help girls not only to solidify their inner lives but also to increase their self-control, cope with disappointment, and be patient through ambiguity. These are the essential factors in a girl's believing that she will prevail and have a life of great purpose.

Tips & Tactics

When your daughter is upset, empathize with her feelings, then focus the dialogue on her ability to take charge: "I can tell you're upset. Have you thought about what you might do next?"

• • •

One way to keep boundaries firm while providing a way for your daughter to be in control is to offer her choices when it comes to setting limits. For example, if her grades are subpar and you want her to spend a few hours studying on the weekend, let her create her weekend schedule.

12. Step by Step
The Process for Success

My seventh-grade Missouri notebook was a beauty. Soft black felt fit snuggly around the front and back covers of the thick compilation of history and photographs about the Show-Me State. The shiny black spiral binding that Dad had installed at the printing company where he worked held it all together. But the pièce de résistance was my mother's contribution. She had glued on sparkling iridescent sequins one by one to outline Missouri's shape on the front cover. I couldn't have been prouder turning in "my" assignment, while in the back of my mind I knew it had been, in part, a family project.

The good news, according to my mom, is that I did create the actual contents without help. Phew. This didn't surprise me. I remember my parents assisting when I got stuck on math problems and my mother typing a few papers for me (actually, many papers for me), but my parents weren't the sort to swoop in and make my life easier when it came to homework.

As reported in the *Wall Street Journal*, teachers are wising up to the fact that the "penetrating report on the Peloponnesian War" wasn't done by a fifth-grade student.[43] Surveys show that parents' reasons for being overly involved in their children's schoolwork include everything from believing that the child is too tired or busy to improving the chances that their offspring will be accepted at top schools.[44] The unintended result, unfortunately, is that young students often fail to learn how to get the job done properly.

Each year as we approach midterm exams at Miss Hall's School, we speak with students, particularly our youngest, about the process of preparing for in-depth assessments. We give girls tips on how to begin, how to sustain the effort, and how to finish the job. That is, we discuss with them an approach that has a beginning, a middle, and an end.

There are very few opportunities in our rush-ahead culture for adolescents to experience *process*, what the dictionary defines as "a particular method of doing something, generally involving a number of steps."[45] Ours is a culture that skips steps (or assigns them to machines). We want results, we want them now, and we have taught our children to want the same things.

The problem is that it is precisely within these steps that we encounter difficulty, dead ends, and frustration. It is only by finding ways around those obstacles that we are able to keep moving toward our goals. Our daughters have no other way of learning how to do this work other than by doing the work. As the saying goes, the only way through it is through it.

Girls need tools in order to be able to work through problems step by step. Just learning how to break up a task into smaller manageable pieces is a basic but elusive life skill for many adolescents. We shouldn't be surprised at this elusiveness, given our culture's fascination with instant gratification. Those born during the latter part of the twentieth century have grown up in a broadband world where very little effort is required to have faster, easier access to almost everything. Our job as parents and teachers is to show girls how to pursue dreams that can't be realized with the click of a mouse.

Planning, organizing, managing, setting priorities, estimating—all these proficiencies take time to teach, time to learn, and time to practice. When we ask a girl what her plan is, when we answer her questions with a question, when we resist the temptation to interrupt the process by doing the job for her, we are helping her to become a resilient problem solver.

Are girls ever just lazy? Of course, and so are we all. Furthermore, the strategy of procrastination knows no age limits. When we are dealing with adolescents, however, the issues of accomplishment and success are inextricably intertwined first with maturity and readiness to embrace the next challenge and then with the learned competencies that make success possible. Sequined report covers notwithstanding, our role as the adults in girls' lives is not to do their assignments but to give our girls the skills for success as well as our whole-hearted belief in their power to achieve.

Tips & Tactics

The first step toward being successful is knowing what success looks like. At the beginning of a new year or prior to your daughter's embarking on a new challenge, ask her to finish the sentence, "I will be successful when . . ." Responses may be similar to the following:

". . . I have maintained a B+ average for one term."

". . . I have made two new friends."

". . . I have made varsity soccer."

Ask her to write down five steps that she will take to move her toward her goal.

13. Girl Talk
Crucial Conversations

Obsessive, constant talk with girlfriends when I was a teen? Sure. How else would I have made it through those years? I would no sooner finish dinner than I'd be on the phone (pink Princess) to girlfriends I'd been with at school just a few hours earlier. There was some studying together, but geometry proofs were set aside more than once so we could solve whatever pressing personal problems had come up that day. On Friday nights we talked on slow drives up and down Main Street or slouched on pillows at sleepovers with Kingston Trio songs playing in the background. If my frustration or confusion seemed inappropriate for my peer group, I called an older mentor, my church choir director, and talked to her.

According to a *New York Times* article, teen girls' obsessive talk (which now includes e-mail, text and instant messaging, and social networking) has captured the attention of researchers.[46] Psychologists have studied what they refer to as *co-rumination*, girls' frequent or obsessive conversations about their problems. The gist of the researchers' findings is that excessive talking can "contribute to emotional difficulties, including anxiety and depression [and that] dwelling [on] and rehashing issues can keep girls . . . stuck in negative thinking patterns."[47] According to one researcher, "When girls are talking about these problems . . . they are not putting two and two together, [and] actually this excessive talking can make them feel worse."[48]

Inferences about girls' talk contributing to their poor mental health raises red flags for me. Those of us who teach girls know that their being in conversation with others at a time in their lives when they are trying to define who they are is not only healthy but as crucial to growing up today as it was forty years ago. For girls, the world coheres through relationships. When it is time to sort out contradictions, test ideas, and work through dilemmas, girls very often do that work in relationship with each other and thus sustain essential connections.

What we are left to think after reading the *New York Times* article is that girls do not know their own minds and thus fall into an abyss of endless, anxiety-producing chatter. This is not necessarily the case. What is true, however, is that as a society we do not socialize girls to speak up and take charge of solving problems. As girls become aware of the rules for success as defined in much of today's culture, they begin to believe that keeping their assertiveness and authenticity in check is what is required. Furthermore, too often we do not structure learning environments in ways that give girls permission to say what is on their minds, to develop the skills associated with robust and respectful dialogue, and, in general, to have control over their own lives.

In the absence of that structure, girls' talk can slide into the ineffective co-rumination the article describes, a function of accepted limitations. With this in mind, I suggest that we focus research not on girls' excessive talk, but on why we as the adults in their lives do not support their developing competency in the skills we know are critical to lives of purpose and fulfillment. Instead of discussing co-rumination, we could be talking about collaboration and teamwork, terms that imply strength and confidence.

The article suggests that we also shortchange girls by asserting, as one psychologist mentioned in the article does, that the primary stressors in girls' lives, those issues that cause them to develop negative thought eddies, are "starting dating or starting serious relationships with boys, concerns about cliques, being popular."[49] Good heavens—is *Sex and the City* now the lens through which we view adolescent growth and development? I'm not suggesting that girls aren't thinking about these topics, but there is so much more that orients a girl as she moves from adolescence into adulthood.

When I asked a Miss Hall's School student for her opinion about these stressors, she said, "The main focus isn't boys, it's on more important things like school, sports, and friends." Then came her key idea: "In this environment you can be yourself, and that levels the playing field." In other words, girls learn and interact in the Miss Hall's School setting on their own terms, not by having to adopt a persona that doesn't fit. As any adult here will tell you, that freedom to be yourself cuts down significantly on all sorts of passive behaviors, including unproductive co-rumination. We can see that in a context of authentic strength, the content as well as the style of girl talk shifts.

The *New York Times* article referred to the American Girl series of books as offering suggestions to girls on problem solving. I applaud those initiatives. Indeed, the part of a girl's education that is concerned with the competencies needed to assume responsibility may be affected by what she reads, the ideas she encounters, or the situations she experiences in stories. However, it is ultimately at their schools and in their homes where girls must be surrounded by environments that support their growth. As the adults in girls' lives, we need to understand that the true stressors for them are related to their being themselves and their knowing that their authenticity will be accepted and valued. Our daughters need to know that they have our permission for authenticity, our validation for uniqueness, and our support for learning how to take charge of their changing lives. That is something for girls to talk about.

Tips & Tactics

The teen years are when girls should be learning how to make decisions based on their personal ideals and values. As your daughter processes the dilemmas in her life, listen for any indication that she is trading her authenticity, or what she genuinely believes is right and true, for acceptance by her peer group. If you sense that happening, engage her in a conversation and confirm her ideas. Perhaps you can also share a story of your own about a time when you stood up for what you believed and how you managed a negative response from others. Learning how to have the courage of one's convictions takes practice and a parent's support.

14. Eye to Eye
Direct Engagement

It may have been a test I failed or a paper that wasn't up to par. Whatever it was precisely, it was a serious academic shortfall that brought me to a meeting with my seventh-grade English teacher, a situation I hadn't faced before. I remember walking up to her desk, and then something strange started happening to my eyes. Reflecting back, I think I may have been crossing them, but at the time it felt involuntary. Whatever I did allowed me not to see the teacher's face. Because of my eye contortions, she was nothing more than a big blur. As a result, I didn't have to look at the disappointment on her face, and I could mitigate my shame.

Looking the other way, avoiding direct eye contact, covering one's face, or in my case, distorting my vision are all responses to shame, embarrassment, fear, and anger. We know how difficult it can be even for us as adults to look at someone directly when we are humiliated or agitated or when we must confront an issue. For teens it is even harder. Most adolescents opt for looking down at the ground or staring straight ahead through the car's front windshield when talking about issues that are emotionally charged.

For adolescent girls, multiply these tendencies by ten. Our daughters are hardwired to detect others' reactions almost instantly. In her book *The Female Brain*, psychiatrist Louann Brizendine says that "the female brain is gifted at quickly assessing the thoughts, beliefs, and intentions of others, based on the smallest hints."[50] In fact, writes Brizendine, compared to boys, "girls . . . arrive in the world better at reading faces and hearing emotional tones."[51] Furthermore, anyone who spends time around a teen girl is most likely familiar with how sensitive a girl can be to any reaction she perceives as negative or critical. Brizendine explains that it is the "new hormonal surges" at this time in a girl's life that "assure that all of her female-specific brain circuits will become even more sensitive to emotional nuance, such as approval and disapproval, acceptance and rejection."[52] Learning to engage with others directly and to sustain strong eye contact when all emotional receptors are in overdrive, therefore, can be a challenge for girls just at the time when developing these skills is essential.

Perhaps what is most effective in encouraging these skills is the influence of an environment that gives girls permission to be their strong, authentic selves. Every year recent graduates return to campus after a semester or two in college and report that they can spot other young women who have graduated from all-girls schools and that professors often identify them as alumnae of these schools. These students exhibit a relaxed and direct approach to engaging with others and a confidence in expressing personal opinions. I am reminded of a quote from Annie Dillard's novel *The Maytrees*: "Under her high brows she eyed him straight on and straight across. She had gone to girls' schools, he recalled later. Those girls look straight at you."[53]

We want girls to develop comfort with direct engagement by learning to be reflective and to question what gets in the way. We teach a girl to ask herself why she reacts the way she does to certain situations and to identify the sources of her feelings. During my conversation last year with a student leader, the girl asked, "Why is it almost painful for me to have to tell another girl that she is out of dress code?" As we continued our conversation, the student answered the question for herself. "I put myself in her shoes and project how that comment would make me feel." In other words, empathy was causing the girl to shy away from the conversation she needed to have. The solution, this student leader decided, was for her to create a few phrases that would allow her to be more comfortable dealing with the issue. For example, it was easier for her to initiate the conversation by opening with the question, "Do you know you're out of dress code?"

Susan Scott, author of the book *Fierce Conversations: Achieving Success in Work and Life, One Conversation at a Time* and executive coach for Fortune 500 companies, says that relationships are our most valuable currency and that "the conversation *is* the relationship."[54] Furthermore, according to Scott, "The most powerful communications technology any of us will ever have is eye contact."[55] Our young women will have authentic, respectful, and productive conversations in the future because they have had the opportunity to practice looking people in the eye and using their voices with confidence.

Tips & Tactics

Give your daughter the opportunity to practice engaging in difficult conversations. When there are issues to be resolved with a teacher or a peer, role-play with her so she can practice what she will say. If the conversation is to be with an adult, you can accompany your daughter and provide moral support, but let her do the talking.

• • •

Girls can easily adopt passive-aggressive ways to deal with conflict. The eye roll, the disgusted look, silence, and moodiness are all behaviors that a girl may indulge in when she is angry or resistant to what is happening. Dismissing those behaviors with a girls-will-be-girls attitude shortchanges your daughter. When you see passive-aggressive behavior in her, acknowledge her upset, then ask her to tell you what she wants you to know. When she does, be ready to avoid taking her words personally. Engage calmly with her toward the goal of a negotiated outcome.

15. Cranky Chronicles
Anger and Conflicting Expectations

Over the holidays, Mom and I were chatting happily in the kitchen when out of the blue she said, "Did I tell you that awhile back I found a bunch of your hate letters?" I had been doing some last-minute baking while we talked. That came to a halt. "What hate letters?" I asked, now giving her my full attention. "The ones you wrote when you were a teenager, telling me how much you hated me." Good grief. She seemed to be amused by the whole topic. I was thinking that there should be a law against dredging up stuff like this after forty years.

I have no memory of writing the incriminating letters, but I do remember pouring out my frustrations into a small green diary. I had several good friends with whom I thrashed through adolescent angst over the phone or at slumber parties, but the diary was also a safe place to vent. I kept it locked and hidden away (and it still is, in my basement).

Things have changed. Whereas I tucked my private thoughts away in a bottom drawer (except for the recently discovered letters), teens today share their thoughts with millions on social networking websites. Adolescents chronicle everything about their lives, from their daily schedules to personal frustrations with peers and parents. As author Emily Nussbaum has observed about this phenomenon, "[It's] as if a generation were given a massive technological truth serum. . . . The private experience of adolescence . . . has been made public."[56]

A quick recall of the examples we provide for young people—reality TV, talk shows that showcase every social taboo, teen idols who broadcast the most intimate details of their lives—makes us wonder why we are surprised that adolescents tell all. However, what is most interesting from a gender perspective about this explosion in Internet-based truth telling is that it provides an outlet for teen aggression. The hostile language some girls use in this web-based hideout would stupefy most parents.

What is this about? We know girls get angry. They are frustrated for all the reasons teens have been frustrated for generations—not enough freedom and too many rules. But there is another source of teenage angst for girls, one that is related to our conflict as a society about what it means to be a girl.

It is still, as it was in my youth, unacceptable for a girl to display anger. Being nice and perfect continues to have great currency for girls in our culture. Rachel Simmons, in her book *Odd Girl Out: The Hidden Culture of Aggression in Girls*, reminds us that "females are expected to mature into caregivers, a role deeply at odds with aggression," adding that "aggression is the hallmark of masculinity."[57] Author Peggy Orenstein has quoted psychologists Lyn Mikel and Carol Gilligan, who described the "perfect girl" as one who "has no bad thoughts or feelings, the kind of person everyone wants to be with . . . the girl who speaks quietly, calmly, who is always nice and kind, never mean or bossy."[58]

That said, today more girls than ever before have ample opportunities to fulfill their potential. They aspire to careers unimaginable to those of us of my generation. So, on the one hand, we advise girls, live your dreams. But, as a society, we add, do it quietly, without calling too much attention to yourself. As Simmons says, "We are telling girls to be bold and timid, voracious and slight, sexual and demure."[59] When a girl tries to hold such contradictions inside, she naturally experiences conflict and anger.

Unsure about how to integrate natural feelings of competition, ambition, and jealousy with the convoluted feminine ideals in our culture, girls become frustrated and often believe they have no choice but to take their anger underground. In online diaries and wherever the teen culture goes below adult radar, girls often manifest their conflict through aggressive language. And just as society often uses hateful terms to describe assertive girls and women, girls can find themselves using the same language about each other.

The answer is to support girls in their above-the-radar talk, to help them work through the very real conflicts in which they find themselves, and to give them an image of what a fully realized woman can be like. When we are committed to allowing girls to give voice to their frustrations in this way, they do not have to displace their feelings onto each other. Instead, they can learn to feel powerful themselves.

Tips & Tactics

Teach your daughter how to use the "When you . . . . I feel . . ." strategy of communicating.

For example, "When you . . .

> . . . tell me what to wear . . .

> . . . set a curfew . . .

> . . . tell me I can't go to the party . . .

I feel . . .

> . . . like a two-year old."

> . . . like I can't have any fun."

> . . . like you don't trust me."

Your being able to hear this language and your willingness to stay engaged in conversation give your daughter invaluable practice in finding appropriate and authentic ways to confront difficulty.

• • •

Encouraging your daughter to speak out in respectful ways to voice dissent does not mean that she must prevail and get her way. If the party she wants to attend is unsupervised, your answer will still be no, but your daughter has been able to practice asserting herself and being able to accept no as an answer.

16. The Tangled Web We Weave
Understanding Teen Deception

I was in the shower back at the cabins, having been for a swim at YoCoMo church camp one August in the late fifties. Suddenly, I was aware that someone was calling my name, both first and last. "Is Jeannie Jensen in here?" "Yes," I answered nervously. The response came back, "You're in big trouble—the whole camp has been searching for you." Hair dripping wet, towel hastily wrapped around me, my face flushing bright red, I stepped out to see the camp counselor, looking grim. "You didn't sign out when you left the pool," she said. Detail escapes me, but I do remember my confusion at that moment about whether or not I had done what was required. The growing awareness that every camper and counselor on the grounds was looking for me (and talking about me) led to overwhelming embarrassment, and my mind scrambled to come up with an explanation. Finally, I blurted out, "I think I asked a friend to do that." It was a medium-sized trauma for me as a young teen, and deception was a technique I grabbed hold of to get through it.

Results of a study by University of Portsmouth (United Kingdom) researcher Vasudevi Reddy show that infants as young as six or seven months old engage in, as Reddy describes it, "subtle manipulations of their own and others' actions, which succeed in deceiving others at least temporarily."[60] She goes on to say that "fake crying is one of the earliest forms of deception to emerge, and infants use it to get attention even though nothing is wrong."[61] Aha! I admit that I used to stand outside my daughters' nursery, peeking through the crack in the door (as Reddy's researchers did), to see if there really was something amiss or if my daughters' crying was a ruse.

Reddy's work is part of ongoing research about the brain size of primates, human and nonhuman. Since the late 1980s, there has been growing interest in what has been called the *Machiavellian intelligence hypothesis* regarding brain development.[62] The term, introduced by researchers Richard Byrne and Andrew Whiten, became a "banner" for several hypotheses promoting the notion that intelligence is "linked with social living and the problems of complexity it can pose."[63] The idea is that there were "spiralling increases in intelligence" as primates developed the capacity to engage in social manipulation, deception, and cooperation in order to deal with the social complexity inherent in many primate groups.[64]

It all sounds complicated, and it is. If we stop for a moment to reflect on our own or our children's development, however, we can accept the fact that humans acquire other higher-order skills (such as thinking abstractly, understanding ambiguity, and analyzing data) gradually and in ways that are mostly unconscious. For example, although I don't recall specifics, there were times when as a teenager I wanted the keys to the car. Mom might say, "Do you like my hair this way?" Almost subconsciously, I'm certain, I would intuit that if I endorsed the new hairstyle, my chances of getting the keys to the car would be better. Whether I liked the new look wasn't the issue, transportation was, so I said what I thought would work.

Reddy points out that we shouldn't attach malevolence or a moral significance to the behavior of infants and toddlers.[65] As she explains, they use deception, which takes many forms and includes fake crying, pretend laughing, concealing forbidden activities, and distracting parents' attention, in order to learn about social interactions, or what does and does not work.[66]

Much of this also is applicable when dealing with teens. Those who have experience teaching adolescents have observed that teens deceive for many reasons, such as to save face, assert autonomy, regain control, be noticed, and as in the case of younger children, find out what works. Obviously, we want girls to be forthright and to engage honestly with others. To support their growth in this direction, as parents and teachers we need to look beyond the deception to what might be motivating a girl to mislead. We must be careful, for example, not to shower too much attention on a girl when she complains, lest we teach her that we are more responsive to grumbling than we are to healthier ways of coping.

As a girl reenters the academic arena each fall, she needs to make adjustments to a greater academic workload, to new friends and teachers, or to unfamiliar living arrangements. In the process, parents can anticipate that a daughter may revert to well-practiced strategies of misleading ("I haven't had a thing to eat for days"), exaggerating ("Everyone hates me"), and withholding information ("There's absolutely nothing to do here"). When that happens, it is essential that parents ask their daughter to reassess the situation and provide a more precise description of what she is experiencing. To do anything else only delays a teen's progression from using old ways of getting what she wants to learning new skills for facing challenges directly and for persevering to reach her goals.

Tips & Tactics

When a teen uses deception to cope with difficulty, we must confront her and help her understand why she chose to lie instead of telling the truth. For example, a parent might say, "I'm sorry that you felt you could not tell me the truth. Can you help me understand why you thought that you had to lie?" We must be ready to hear what our daughters have to say. When a girl can share her feelings without fear, the door is open to having a meaningful conversation about the value of preserving trust.

17. May I Help You?
Cultivating Empathy

My eldest daughter was eight months old and just beginning to walk. She would gently fling herself from one piece of furniture to the next, always making sure there was something sturdy to grab onto. One day we were upstairs, and I was not feeling well. I must have had a bug, because all I wanted to do was to get in bed and stay there. Suddenly, I felt a little pat on my back. Balancing with one hand on a chair and the other on me, my daughter intuited at her very young age that I needed her care. She *empathized* with my misery.

Daniel Goleman writes in his book *Emotional Intelligence: Why It Can Matter More Than IQ* that the roots of empathy can be traced to infancy.[67] However, the ability to sustain and develop our early leanings toward sympathizing with others' pain is not something that happens automatically, like adult teeth replacing the baby versions. If it did, there would be less suffering in the world. Empathy, it turns out, is a capacity that must be nurtured and encouraged, and as individuals we begin to do so by looking inward. According to Goleman, "Empathy builds on self-awareness."[68] He goes on to say that "the more open we are to our own emotions, the more skilled we will be in reading feelings."[69]

Becoming more self-aware is, of course, a major part of the broad curriculum for teens. As parents and educators, our goals for adolescent girls are for them to understand their own moods and to have tried-and-true strategies for resisting overwhelming worry and setbacks. For a girl to remain steady in the storm requires that she have a strong sense of her authentic self. When, with the help of adults who deal with girls honestly and wisely, she achieves greater certainty about who she is and what she values, she can more easily understand and acknowledge the feelings of others. As Goleman points out, "Failure to register another's feelings . . . is a tragic failing in what it means to be human."[70]

Furthermore, writes Goleman, "The root of caring stems from . . . the capacity for empathy."[71] The ability to walk in another's shoes is what makes caring possible. Although girls may have been socialized from the time they were young to be caregivers, it is during the high-school years that this impulse acquires depth. Programs like Horizons, Miss Hall's School's community-service, experiential-learning program, allow girls to deepen their understanding of the human condition and to grow confident that they can make a positive difference. It is this type of experience that allows a girl to begin to define what caring for others will mean for her. Over time, she will grasp how she can change a small corner of the world, if not the world itself.

Over many years, the Miss Hall's School community has come together to respond to catastrophic world events that have caused widespread suffering. Girls have taken the lead on these many occasions in creating ways for the community to reach out to the victims of hurricanes, tsunamis, and earthquakes, whether here in the United States or in places around the globe. Each time, girls have experienced firsthand the challenges of executing plans successfully as well as the thrill of feeling competent when they got the job done.

Our work as parents and educators is not finished, however, if we stop at encouraging greater self-awareness and at teaching girls how to translate feelings of empathy into action. We also want girls to move forward during these high-school years to think beyond caring and charity to the larger issue of the causes of human suffering. What are the conditions that lead to the need for charity? How can we distinguish between Shakespeare's "thousand natural shocks that flesh is heir to," which demand one type of response, and issues of justice?[72] To paraphrase a parable, charity is rescuing people from the river as they are being carried downstream; justice is stopping what caused them to fall into the river in the first place.[73] We are educating the next generation of global leaders, young women who will be empathic, analytical, and competent, to take action. Our goal is for them to convert their desire to help, as in the case of my eight-month-old daughter, into an ability to create a better, more just world.

Tips & Tactics

Girls benefit enormously by interacting with others who do not share their background and beliefs. If your daughter's school does not provide a diverse population, seek other venues in the community where she can get involved. She develops self-awareness and empathy when she learns others' stories and can think about how her own story is related.

18. Just Like Us
Belonging to a Global Family

What was good for one was good for all in my little group of high-school friends, and that extended to vocal study with Mr. Sovereign. He paid me fifty cents an hour to accompany the voice lessons he gave to dozens of students, including four of my best friends. Part of each lesson was devoted to using *solfeggio* (do, re, mi, and so on) to sing Concone (an Italian composer) vocal exercises. One couldn't look at the book; it all had to be memorized. Since my back was to Mr. Sovereign, he couldn't see me, and when my friends would have a momentary brain freeze, I would silently mouth the syllables until they got back on track. Today I am clear that my assistance was ethically questionable. At the time, however, it seemed to be exactly what was needed so that we could *all* (I studied, too) get an "Excellent!" written in our lesson books for that week.

I was reminded of the one-for-all and all-for-one approach not long ago when I invited members of the Miss Hall's School Environmental Club into my office. Earlier in the year, they had sent me a proposal for installing energy-efficient motion sensors to control the lights in the bathrooms around campus. By the time I read the girls' proposal, they had purchased one sensor, tested it to gauge its effectiveness, and determined that the plan would work. Their proposal challenged me to match the

$769 they had raised so that sensors could be installed throughout the campus. Needless to say, I said yes immediately. Now, meeting in my office with the girls, I wanted to hear how they came up with the idea and how they were able to bring their project to such a successful conclusion.

The girls discussed how they divided the work of finding the best product for the best price. Their faculty advisor had convinced them that they would have a better chance of getting a nod from me if they knew exactly what the project would cost, had raised some of the funds themselves, and had tested the concept to know that it would work. After that, they agreed that it was the passion they all shared about the need to conserve resources that kept them moving along. I told them that when I was their age, I would never have thought of such a project. They responded by saying that their generation is keenly interested in conservancy because, as one girl said, "It affects everyone." In other words, no country exists in isolation from an environmental perspective. One girl added, "When it comes to sustainability, it won't be a healthy environment for any of us until it's a healthy environment for all."

Brava to these young women who understand that we are only as strong as the weakest among us! Too often, adults who should know better focus only on one part of the population. They view the status of girls in this country through a narrow lens and make the grand pronouncement that in this post-Title IX, equal-employment-opportunity age, all is well for our daughters and young women. However, all is not well for every girl in this country. One only has to remember the number of children living in poverty (18.9 percent in 2009) or the hundreds of thousands of children estimated to be at risk of becoming victims of commercial sexual exploitation.[74]

For a global perspective, we just have to click on the Human Rights Watch website. Although the following excerpt refers to women specifically, we know that girls worldwide are also at great risk: "Millions of women throughout the world live in conditions of abject deprivation of, and attacks against, their fundamental human rights for no other reason than that they are women. . . . Violence and discrimination against women are global social epidemics."[75]

As parents and educators, we are committed to helping girls to develop deep empathy for others and to understand that their individual lives do not reflect the reality of the vast majority of their peers around the world. As long as girls anywhere are starving, abused, or denied access to health care and education, all cannot be well with our own daughters. A former Miss Hall's School student body president summed it up well in referring to the student council's Penny Wars Project, which raised over $1,400 to benefit a girls' school in Kibera, one of Kenya's largest slums: "Those girls are just like us, trying to learn, but they have so little. How can we not help?"

Tips & Tactics

Engage in conversations with your daughter about the reality of girls, both here and abroad, who are exploited and deprived of an education. Ask her how she would spend a million dollars if it all had to be used to relieve the suffering of children around the world.

19. She's Got High Hopes
Expectations in a Changing Society

When I was in the seventh grade, Mom went to work. Until then, she had always been at home, volunteering in our church and my schools, but first and foremost in charge of my brother, me, and our house. Although she had been a buyer for a department store in Kansas City before she and Dad were married, her venture back into the work world was to help my dad, part time, in a small business he was running when I was young. I didn't see my mother as a career woman. She was Mom, who left home a few hours a day while I was at school to help Dad out and add a few dollars to the family income.

My daughters, on the other hand, saw a mom *and* a career woman when they looked my way. It was the early seventies, and the women's movement had set sail. As a generation of women, we were entering uncharted waters, and I was not alone, I suspect, in feeling as though one foot was left on the shore. Managing dishes and diapers was a snap; I had watched Mom in action for years. But adding job deadlines to dishes, diapers, and day care gave a whole new meaning to the term *multitasking*. Indeed, not only was it a hassle filling the Crock-Pot and getting out the door with two children in tow, it was also a challenge figuring out who I would be when I arrived at work.

I had prepared for a career by earning credentials and degrees. But composing a persona that could participate, have influence, shape outcomes, and move easily in a dynamic work world turned out to be a true test. As Smith College President Carol Christ wrote in the *Smith Alumnae Quarterly*, "Degrees and credentials in hand, educated women in the '60s and '70s entered a professional workplace whose gender composition was changing rapidly. . . . Roughly from 1970 to 1980, women's expectations about the role of work in their lives evolved dramatically."[76]

It is understandable that many of my generation struggled early in their careers with the notion of being able to contribute in significant ways to the larger environment beyond the home. After all, stepping into that work world had been described to some of us as "something you might need to do to earn extra money" or "something to fall back on if, God forbid, something horrible happens." In my case, it took time and a reordering of my most deeply held assumptions to be comfortable with the idea that I was passionate about my chosen work and that I had a vision for change.

Now we understand, as Christ goes on to point out, that it is women from the sixties and seventies who are "creating . . . the world for which we, today, are preparing [our] daughters."[77] Our young women will be greeted by a more welcoming climate than we encountered, one with more opportunities and role models. However, the biggest shift from then to now is in the expectations our daughters will take with them when they step out of adolescence into adult lives of purpose. They will expect to sit at the table and even to change the shape of the table if necessary.

Girls here at Miss Hall's School know, furthermore, that we look to them to suggest a better way and propose new directions wherever they see the need. They expect to be valued for their contributions, so they also will expect that response in the future. In elected and informal leadership roles on campus, girls assume they will be heard and taken seriously, so they also will assume those reactions when they move into adulthood.

Without a doubt, our daughters will find in their quest to be full participants that considerable societal change is needed. The data confirm that the playing fields are nowhere near level in corporate and business sectors. According to the *2010 Catalyst Census* from the nonprofit research group Catalyst, just 15.7 percent of board seats and 14.4 percent of executive officer positions in Fortune 500 companies are held by women.[78] As for elected office, the leadership gap between women and men is huge in the United States. Closing that gap will take skill and stamina. Finally, but most importantly, a transformation needs to occur in America's workplaces to make it possible for women *and* men to parent their children *and* to contribute to a robust and vibrant economy.

Where there is need, there is opportunity. As I watch girls lead change here, I know beyond a doubt that our daughters will seize the opportunity to shape a new world for themselves and their children and to lead us all into a more enlightened future.

Tips & Tactics

At least once a month, ask your daughter to describe some action she took that led to an improved outcome for herself and others. Perhaps she made the assist that allowed her team to win the game or suggested to a group of friends that they all have lunch with a new girl at school. Girls are leading change all the time, but unless we help them reflect on what they have done, they can miss seeing themselves as making a difference.

20. Success with Integrity
Girls and Perceptions of Ambition

There were nearly five hundred students at Joplin Senior High School when I was enrolled there in the sixties, but the group I took classes and hung out with numbered about thirty. Not having Advanced Placement courses available, we vied for spots in accelerated classes. In Mr. Stewart's junior English class, the tension hung in the air as we all struggled to be the first to have an epiphany about the symbolism in a Walt Whitman poem. We worried about our GPAs, worked late into the night on assignments, and breathed a sigh of relief when we were inducted into the National Honor Society and invited to Joplin Electric Company to receive our Reddy Kilowatt academic achievement pins. In other words, we were in a dead heat for top academic honors, but the conversation among the girls in the group never betrayed a hint of competition.

In fact, I clearly remember that my girlfriends and I downplayed our accomplishments. "How did you do on the algebra test?" someone would ask. "I'm sure I bombed it," would be the reply. A grade of A on a paper was never announced to friends. Instead, one would say something like, "I didn't do too badly; he must have given everyone extra points." Not only were we not comfortable discussing our achievements, but asserting personal ambition and being ambitious for each other was not something that ever would have entered our minds.

Although it has been decades since those high-school days, there is still much ambivalence in our culture about competition, ambition, assertiveness, and achievement in relation to girls and women. When Rosa Parks died, columnist Ellen Goodman wrote an article titled "The Mythology of Rosa Parks," in which she pointed out that Parks was a "civil rights activist long before that fateful bus ride."[79] Goodman went on to say, however, that Parks is often lauded as a "humble seamstress," an unassuming woman who with quiet dignity but no political ambition simply refused to give up her seat on the bus.[80] "Is this how we praise women? As unambitious, accidental heroines?" Goodman asked, adding, "How does the political imperative to be ambitious gel with the cultural imperative to be 'unassuming'?"[81]

Around the time of the anniversary of Parks's historical refusal, I took the Goodman article to an all-school meeting here at Miss Hall's School. Our mission and mantra, as the girls know well, is that those in this school today will make change for good in the world tomorrow. Parks is just one more example of someone who, through her bold courage and willingness to risk discomfort, changed a nation. I wanted the girls to reflect on those personal qualities.

Furthermore, I knew from some of the girls on the Girls' Leadership Project research team that discussions about girls' support for each other in leadership roles were under way. Goodman had included a comment in her article that was relevant. "Indeed, sometimes women are better at providing support for each other's disappointments than ambitions," she wrote, "better at offering comfort than at urging risk."[82]

Girls are aware that there is a conflict between competitiveness and caring in the societal psyche regarding women in leadership. The question for girls is how to incorporate both qualities simultaneously. This question prompted a series of conversations that included all of the students in the school. They are not alone in exploring these topics. Nan Mooney, author of *I Can't Believe She Did That! Why Women Betray Other Women at Work*, was quoted in a *USA Today* article as saying that the way that we socialize girls to get along and not make waves results in women who believe that the only way to have a healthy relationship is to "have a positive relationship and be nice."[83] Then, according to Mooney, "we get into the workplace, and it's competitive."[84] The result, according to several women quoted in the article, is that problems "go underground" and the work environment can become "perplexing" and "duplicitous."[85]

Not everyone agrees that women and men compete differently. Furthermore, saying that women have trouble working with each other draws criticism that one is, as Mooney herself says, anti-woman.[86] The issue of girls and women supporting each other in leadership roles, nonetheless, is an important topic and one we should encourage our daughters to continue to explore. In the end, however, how one interacts with others is largely a matter of personal integrity, as one Miss Hall's School student stated so well. "I want to be competitive, but I want to do the right thing with other people," she said. She added, "The question is, how far are you willing to go to get something without sacrificing your concern for others?"

Tips & Tactics

Talk with your daughter about who holds elected leadership roles in her school. Are girls in those roles? Do girls aspire to leadership? Does your daughter want to head a club or be a class officer? If you hear ambivalence from her about her desire to seek a leadership role, try to find out why she feels this way. Is it because she fears that she will fail in her attempt to be elected? Does she believe she will not be able to do the job? Does she fear that she will be a target for criticism? By teasing out the issues behind your daughter's resistance, you support her in confronting her unwillingness to take the healthy risks that life requires of all of us.

21. The Double Bind
Asserting Leadership Skills

The high-school youth group at church was preparing the program for Christmas Eve. I don't remember my title, but I was in charge of making sure we were ready. It's too long ago to recall the details about what was amiss, but the gist is that some of the other kids (boys) weren't listening and, in general, were not much interested in respecting my leadership. There wasn't anything particularly unusual about that. It was the early sixties. Girls led only in a few places, churches being one.

What is still a vivid memory, however, is the action of one boy in the group. A year or two older, Norman Fretwell was a leader, respected by all, handsome, and one of the highest-ranking ROTC students at the high school. Just at the moment when it looked as though the meeting would disintegrate into confusing disorder, Norman spoke up. "We all need to listen to Jeannie," he said. "She has a good plan, and we need to get this done." That was all it took. Norman had spoken. From then on, there were no problems.

I'm sure there were a hundred things wrong with the way I presented myself in that meeting so many years ago. Not only was I not comfortable with my personal authority back then, I didn't know I had personal authority. Perhaps I was speaking too softly, or not being clear, or projecting uncertainty. For whatever reason, I was not seen as a leader. Although many years have passed since that church meeting, young women still struggle to develop an effective leadership style and to be taken seriously.

One factor that contributes to this struggle is the shortage of role models. Certainly in the United States, the emergence of women leaders has been more of a steady trickle than a surging stream over the decades since I was a teen. Girls still can't look at our society and see gender represented at levels that make a significant impact. Therefore, providing girls and young women with "glimpses of what [they] might become," to use scholar Herminia Iabarra's phrase, is essential.[87]

Girls here at Miss Hall's School have the advantage of seeing a range of leadership styles, not only among the women and men who work here and among visiting alumnae, but also among their peers. Our students therefore develop a context for thinking about what leadership is and broaden their definition to include, as one student said, "asking others to quiet down in the library" or "inspiring someone to paint."[88]

There is more to developing confidence in asserting oneself than having sufficient role models, however. In a *Wall Street Journal* article, author Erin White referenced leadership experts who say that young women managers must "navigate a 'double-bind.'"[89] "If they assert themselves forcefully," she writes, "people may perceive them as not acting feminine enough, triggering a backlash."[90] But if they try a more feminine approach, she adds, "they aren't seen as strong leaders."[91] White describes the conundrum using the words of one newly minted manager who was "preoccupied with wanting to be seen as nice," and who was "uncomfortable having to give negative feedback."[92]

Girls understand the double bind, and throughout the teen years they wrestle with the challenges of how to integrate their becoming independent with their staying in relationship with family members and peers. As psychologist Lori Stern concludes from her work with adolescent girls, "Relationships without independence become just as problematic as independence without relationships."[93] In this school setting, we see the struggle when we notice girls attempting to assert what they know is right while factoring in what others will think about what they say and what type of response they will get.

Our work to support girls in bridging these competing priorities is rooted in our belief that, as Stern writes, "independence . . . involves the renegotiation and reframing of relationships."[94] To do that reframing, a girl must learn the skills that will allow her to stay in relationships while speaking and acting in ways that are consistent with her personal values. Competency in these skills is essential to true leadership.

As parents and teachers, we cannot guarantee that our young women will be taken seriously in every instance. We have confidence, however, that with our guidance, they will have a head start in knowing how to assert themselves authentically and effectively in their personal and professional lives.

Tips & Tactics

Ask your daughter whom she admires and why. Adults as well as peers provide girls with examples, both positive and negative, of how to live one's life. Suggest that your daughter make a list of real-life heroes (not celebrities) and that after each name she add three reasons the person is on the list.

22. Voice Lessons
Confirming the Value of Words

Trouble was brewing at my hometown church, the church in which I grew up. A schism had developed, and two factions were at odds. One, led by the preacher, was preparing to exit the congregation. I was a young teen at the time, and I can see myself walking with a few adults out the side door of the building as church members were discussing whether they would stay or leave. I had absorbed the ideas swirling around me, and in a moment of unusual risk taking, I echoed the position my parents were taking, one that I thought made sense. I said to a man three times my age, "You should stay. The church is the people, not the person who preaches on Sunday."

I remember that I surprised myself. I hadn't heard my assertive voice much. It was the fifties in southwest Missouri, and adults were not in the habit of asking anyone younger than twenty what she thought. When I read an article in the *Smith Alumnae Quarterly* not long ago, I was reminded of this event. The author, a Smith graduate, had seen the "faces of presence and possibility" when she had attended the graduation of her goddaughter from Smith, and she made the case in her essay for why she believes that the all-women setting is, as she wrote, "still urgently needed."[95] One of her points caught my attention: "Smith develops voice, not echo."[96]

Mira Hall, the founder of Miss Hall's School, was one of the earliest graduates of Smith College, and her experience there undoubtedly inspired her to create an environment at her school for girls that had some of the same transformational properties as her alma mater. At Miss Hall's School, girls indeed learn to speak out. In fact, *finding her voice* is a frequently used metaphor here to describe those moments when a girl realizes not only that she has something to say but also that we are anxious to hear it.

A girl's voice may first come out, as mine did, as an echo. It takes time, after all, for a girl to develop opinions and insights that are consistent with her deep interior promptings. It also takes time for a girl to summon the courage to risk putting a stake in the ground and to say, "This is what I believe." Our work as parents and as teachers in supporting her in that great enterprise is to engage with her. We must confirm the value of her words. ("I'm glad you mentioned that.") We must validate. ("Perceptive insight. Did everyone hear that?") We must encourage more. ("Please elaborate. I'm eager to know why you think that.") In other words, we are here to help her find the expression that is authentically hers, which then will lead her to knowing that her contributions matter and that her leadership is needed.

In her commencement address to Wellesley College graduates a few years ago, Madeleine Albright said that leadership is often misunderstood. "We expect it to come from the outside," she explained, "[and] so we wait and listen for the sound of some mighty voice coming out of a loud speaker."[97] "Real leadership," she continued, "comes from the quiet nudging of an inner voice."[98] That inner voice is stirred in girls when we listen intently to their agenda, challenge them to stretch beyond what they think they know, and encourage their narration of what they think might be possible in their lives. By helping a girl sense the power of her inner voice, we hope to help her learn to develop it as a reliable compass throughout her life.

Some months ago, a member of the class of 2005 sent me an e-mail with the subject line, "Girls' Voices." She wrote that a recent Verizon ad, despite its purpose of selling her a product, had left her "feeling inspired and empowered."[99] When I clicked on the link, I saw a young woman who said, "Air has no prejudice." This image was followed by a parade of young women, each speaking with confidence as she appeared on the screen: "My ideas will be powerful if they are wise" . . . "infectious" . . . "worthy." "If my thoughts have flawless delivery, I can lead the army that will follow."[100]

What captured this alumna's attention were the messages about the strength of a young woman's ideas and her capacity to have influence and lead change. She recognized the ideas, which were vivid and personally compelling, because she had honed her inner voice in the context of those very same ideas while a student at the school. When we encourage a teen girl to express what she most deeply believes, we confirm the value of her perspective. When we engage with her in thoughtful discussions, we teach her how to refine her thinking and reshape her message. The more we listen and respond to a girl, the more her statements become voice, not echo.

Tips & Tactics

Look for opportunities to confirm the value of your daughter's ideas:

"I'm glad you mentioned that."

"That's an important point."

Validate her comments:

"What a perceptive insight."

"You are on target with that comment."

Encourage her to develop her ideas:

"Please elaborate. I'm eager to know more."

"Tell me why you believe that."

PART TWO:

Parenting with Perspective

23. Who's in Charge?
Confident Parenting

Surely anyone with a sibling remembers the car rides and the bickering. When we were young, my brother and I sat in the back seat on long trips, and it didn't take much for us to become involved in a full-blown squabble. Mom would scold from the front, "You two behave." We'd quiet down for a few minutes, then one of us would poke the other, and it all started up again. Mom would try the distraction approach. "Look out the window and see how many cows you can count," she would suggest. Quiet for a while, another poke, ever so slight, but enough for Tom or me to snap back with a "Stop that!" And then, from the front seat, Dad would bark, "Cut it out!" That reminder of his authority was what we were waiting for. We stopped. No debate, no long, drawn-out negotiation, no coaxing with the reward of a treat if we quieted down. Mom and Dad were in charge, and the bickering needed to stop.

My parents were comfortable being parents. They set limits, managed the challenges that came along (which took more and more courage, I think, as we entered the teen years), and never thought about trying to be our friends. Move forward to my generation, however, and many of us found ourselves quite confused about how to deal with offspring. And it appears that parenting uncertainty continues with the adult children of the baby boomers.

A recent article in the *New Yorker* points out that the newest children's stories routinely reflect parents' confusion and the blurred lines between parent and child. Author Daniel Zalewski provides an enlightening analysis of today's children's books, which "record shifts in domestic life."[101] Using examples from many modern stories, he highlights how parents are being portrayed as befuddled bystanders, hesitant to take a stand when a child "swings upside down on a chandelier and sticks out her tongue" (*Pinkalicious*) or "terrorizes her little brothers" (*Olivia*).[102] Grownups in new children's fiction, he notes, are "easy prey" and "thoroughly steamrolled," and children are the ones with "executive authority."[103]

How did this happen? The flood of advice from so many credentialed professionals, who often disagree, can be bewildering. Maybe our indecision in knowing what to do stems from trying to avoid mistakes we think our parents made. However, I found as I was parenting my daughters that when I lost my grip, it was because I had lost my confidence.

Author and parenting coach Bonnie Harris says that to have the objectivity we need as parents, we must be able to "disengage from the emotions that hijack us [and] take our children's behavior less and less seriously."[104] That, she says, takes a "strong sense of self."[105] I remember the day and moment when I realized that I needed to find a deeper source within me from which to develop the confidence my daughters needed me to have. That work is essential because, as Harris reminds us, our young people cannot feel safe when we are not in charge.[106] Moreover, by the time our girls are teenagers, they need us more than ever to exercise our personal authority so we can help them develop theirs. In other words, feeling powerless as a parent shortchanges our daughters.

The self-adjustments I began to make those many years ago, and that I continue to refine as the parent of my now-grown daughters, are about gaining the confidence to achieve two goals: to avoid taking things personally and to let go of outcomes. First, it is so easy for us, particularly those of us who are mothers, to absorb the emotional content of interactions with girls. We want to rush in and relieve their suffering. We are quick to blame ourselves for their difficulty. We can be awash in guilt before they have even finished describing what's wrong. None of that is helpful. The better plan, I have found, is for me to act from my own quiet center and model the confidence I want my daughters to continue to build in themselves.

Second, our daughters will thrive when we let go of outcomes. Engaging with a girl by acting as a sounding board and asking the questions that will prompt her to reflect and come up with her own solutions is what she needs most. When she can sense that we trust her to be responsible and that we are eager to see her take charge of her life, she can believe in herself. As Harris reminds us, when a girl knows you have nothing at stake in the outcome, "she has the freedom to figure it out."[107]

Sometimes, when I find myself tempted to slip back into old habits of being too prescriptive and judgmental, I hear my dad's words—"Cut it out!"—and I do.

Tips & Tactics

When emotions run high and exchanges with your daughter are heating up, take a deep breath and say to yourself, this is not about me. Even when she may be quite vocal that you are the problem, keep repeating to yourself, this is not about me.

•••

When your daughter is frustrated and out of sorts, lead with questions that signal to her that you are not invested in a specific outcome to her problem. Rather, you want to be available to her if she needs your advice or your reaction to her ideas. For example, you might pose the following questions:

•••

"I can tell how worried you are about the SAT coming up. What are you thinking might give you confidence?"

•••

"I know that making the cut for varsity is important to you. In what areas do you think you have the strongest skills? Have you thought about what you might do if you don't make the cut?"

24. Free-Range Education
Common-Sense Parenting and Teaching

Mom said that she and Dad had me all dressed up, bow in hair, pinafore, white socks, black patent Mary Janes. In her words, "You looked like a doll." I was three years old, and we were at Fisherman's Wharf in San Francisco, headed into a restaurant. My parents momentarily let go of my hand, and I stumbled on the raised threshold and cracked my knee open when I hit the floor. Blood was everywhere. "We had to take you outside to get you presentable again," Mom recalled. She added, "That's when your dad looked at me and said, 'Whatever made us think we could be parents?'"

It was during a call I made to my mom from San Francisco recently that she reminded me of this event. I was taken aback by hearing that Dad ever doubted that he and Mom could be competent parents. As I look back at my childhood, I think of my parents as always knowing what to do. A case in point came up when a colleague and I were recently talking about being bullied as teens. I told her that I remember only one time when a girl at my school was trying to manipulate people and stir up trouble, and it upset me. I went home and told my parents. Dad said, "She shouldn't be doing that," and added, "Just walk away." I remember feeling confirmed in my perceptions that her behavior was wrong, and that gave me the courage to do as Dad said. I had no more problems with the girl.

In the influential 2001 parenting book *The Blessings of a Skinned Knee: Using Jewish Teachings to Raise Self-Reliant Children*, author Wendy Mogel shares her advice about parents needing to step back and give children freedom to grow. The first step, she says, is to "put common sense and faith before emotion."[108] For someone who wondered about his ability to parent, Dad did exactly that. He didn't get caught up in my drama or race out to demand that the school get involved. Instead, he used his common sense to advise me and had faith that I would manage.

There is a movement building to return to using common sense in parenting. In her article "The Growing Backlash against Overparenting," author Nancy Gibbs says parents weary of "obsessing about kids' safety and success" are beginning to embrace "slow parenting" or "free-range parenting," where the message is "less is more."[109] The new campaign is not about "letting your children down," just about restoring balance.[110] In other words, the emphasis is on a return to using our common sense and letting nature take its course, as my parents often said.

In *The Death of Common Sense: How Law Is Suffocating America*, author Philip Howard asserts that government regulations and laws can interfere in a way that "offends common sense."[111] While most of us would acknowledge the enormous safety and health benefits of required seatbelts and smoke-free restaurants, do we really need, as Gibbs noted, the warning label on strollers (Remove Child Before Folding) or the webcams ("Hi, Mom!") in common rooms at college?[112]

I have always believed that one component of our effectiveness in teaching girls here at Miss Hall's School is our preference to use rules judiciously so that we also can rely on our collective good judgment. Whether that inclination stems from the deep wisdom of our founder or from being in New England, where resistance to authority is rooted in the soil, is unclear. Nevertheless, we believe that less is more in teaching girls how to have influence and know their own minds. As a result, girls have the freedom they need to learn how to lead.

Not long ago, we made a change to the school's evening schedule, moving everything up by thirty minutes so that the dormitories could quiet down earlier. The idea had been generated in part by the girls themselves, and they were in full support of the change. The freshwomen, however, the only group with a specific lights-out time, had a concern. Instead of sulking or complaining, they prepared a well-written proposal asking if they could extend the time to "allow us to stay up and finish what we did not get done in study hall." In closing, they wrote, "Thanks for your attention. Please know that you do not necessarily have to accept all parts of the proposal, but please do consider the idea."

Needless to say, we used our collective good sense to cheer the girls' ability to act on their own behalf, and with pleasure we agreed to their request. With a free-range approach to parenting and educating girls, the adults in their lives give them wise counsel and have faith that they will manage.

Tips & Tactics

Sometimes it is our own anxieties that lead to our abandoning our common sense. We project our own worries and fears onto issues, and we lose our perspective. Trusting that you have taught your daughter well and that, therefore, you can have faith that she will act wisely is a good place to begin. Keep that belief in her foremost, take a deep breath when tensions build, and design a way to engage with your daughter to resolve the conflict.

25. Predicting Happiness
Expectations and Reality

Everyone I knew was getting a new binder for school, the kind that was leather and zipped all the way around. We each would stack our books on top of our binder, then balance the pile on one hip as we walked around our junior-high school. I had my heart set on a pink binder I had seen in an office-supply store downtown. A few days before school began, Dad walked through the door carrying a large bag. I knew instantly that he had made the purchase, but when I tore open the package, my heart sank: the binder was brown! Didn't he know that I wanted pink? Then I saw my name engraved in gold letters, and I knew I was stuck. How could I possibly be happy with brown?

It will come as no surprise that I adjusted to brown, and I remember even getting to the point where I preferred the color because I thought it made me look more mature. According to researchers, what I experienced is the norm.[113] Studies of happiness undertaken at major universities have concluded that we are not very good at forecasting our feelings. We "falter when it comes to imagining how we will feel about something in the future."[114] It's not that we don't know that "we will experience visits to Le Cirque and to the periodontist differently," but we tend to overestimate our reaction to both these visits.[115] On average, "bad events proved less intense and more transient . . . [and] good events proved less intense and briefer" than anticipated.[116]

This information has implications for us as parents. Teens have clear ideas about what will make them happy. We can just hear a girl saying, "But I *will* be happy . . . if you'll just give me more allowance . . . if I can have a new roommate . . . if this paper weren't due tomorrow . . . if I could go out tonight with my friends." Since research shows that American parents want their daughters to be happy, we get sucked into the frenzy of trying to meet our own expectations by either caving in to our daughters' demands or feeling bad when we can't.

It's not that a little extra cash wouldn't make an adolescent girl smile. The point the research makes is that the impact of the extra cash is just not as great as a girl predicts that it will be. It is also true that if the parent vetoes the increase, the disappointment will not be as great as the girl and, most likely, the parent anticipate. I wish I had known that when my girls were young!

The explanation for this phenomenon has to do with our ability to acclimate. For example, we adapt quickly to a pleasurable event, according to the research, and "make it the backdrop of our lives."[117] However, the event then becomes ordinary, and "we lose our pleasure."[118] Personal experience tells us this is true, and yet the data confirm that we do not remember that we always adapt. As a result, when happiness with one item fades, we move on to the next and the next, hoping to find permanent bliss. If this is true for adults, imagine how much more so it is for teens.

All this information is important to keep in mind the next time we are toe-to-toe (or phone-to-phone) with an adolescent who is having a bad day and is sure that she knows what will restore happiness. I am not proposing that we quote the research to an emotional teenager, but the data do suggest a few strategies.

First, try to structure a cooling-down period. None of us know what we want when we're in a state of upset. Empathize with your daughter and let her know that you understand her feelings, but suggest that you speak again when she is calmer. As we all know, some crises actually aren't crises at all and will dissipate on their own. When you do talk again, a reality check or data gathering may be in order. If an increase in allowance isn't in the family budget, your daughter needs to hear that. Data gathering, which your daughter (not you) will need to do, will determine whether or not changing roommates or the paper's deadline is possible.

Second, asking your daughter to step back from the immediate issue and recall how she solved a similar problem is another good strategy. Which skills worked for her before? Which ones didn't? We all want our daughters to assemble a toolbox of effective problem-solving strategies. Encourage your daughter to put these thoughts in writing.

Self-knowledge is our goal for our daughters. It takes many of us decades to learn how to move our life choices forward in realistic and sustainable ways. If our daughters learn early on about their reactive patterns, perhaps they won't need to spend so much energy in college, career, and even relationships correcting mistakes. This is something school and parent can teach together.

Tips & Tactics

Suggest to your daughter that she keep a list of the times when she is truly happy. It might be called a TAG (Things Are Good) List or a TUT (Thumbs-Up Times) List. Find a time to discuss the list with her. Chances are that times spent with friends and family members or times spent helping others are what your daughter values most.

• • •

The important thing to remember is that your daughter's disgruntlement does not require that you make her happy.

26. Community Life
The Value of Not Having It All

Riding along in the car some years ago on a ten-day road trip with my husband and my nearly ninety-year-young parents, I had a chance to hear again some family stories. My interest in the Texas Panhandle landscape ran out long before New Mexico appeared, so there was plenty of time for my mother to remind me about her own father's dream to provide his family with a "modern house," a house with indoor plumbing. Dad talked about his parents, who traded their Minnesota farm for a chicken ranch in California. His whole family drove out with a makeshift camper on top of a 1922 Chevy chassis. Christmas, he said, brought no elaborate gifts, just fresh fruit, a rare treat in those days. Rising up through these accounts were the age-old values of hope, courage, hard work, and pride.

As a child, I had more opportunities than my parents had. There were more comfortable-life amenities: indoor plumbing was a given (thank goodness), as were a room of my own and summer vacations. Christmas was a time of plenty. Nonetheless, I watched my parents struggle to make ends meet and to start a family-owned business that went through many lean years before finally succeeding. I witnessed firsthand those same qualities of character that defined my grandparents' lives—lives lived with industry and dignity.

Now I look back and know that it was a gift to see my parents work hard toward their goals. I learned not to take for granted what I was given and not to expect that I would get everything I wanted. I learned to value effort and to persist through the challenges. I learned that the world wouldn't collapse when life got tough.

Segue to the next generation, and I wonder if I made life too easy for my own children. Today's parents have a well-deserved reputation for indulging their offspring emotionally and materially. As reported by Nancy Gibbs in *Time*, polling has found that 80 percent of people think "kids are more spoiled than kids of 10 and 15 years ago, and two-thirds of parents admit that their kids are spoiled."[119] In the same article, Dan Kindlon, author of *Too Much of a Good Thing: Raising Children of Character in an Indulgent Age*, is quoted as saying that "it's not just a little ironic that our success and newfound prosperity—the very accomplishments and good fortune that we so desperately desire to share with our children—put them at risk."[120]

I admit that too often my first instinct was (and still is) to make my daughters' lives perfect. Our daughters may complain when they hit a rough patch, but are we serving them well by removing all obstacles? We can't solve all of their problems, and by trying to, we infantilize daughters and communicate a lack of confidence in their abilities to cope successfully.

No parent sets out to stunt a daughter's emotional growth. We have good intentions, but we don't stop to think what our actions convey. We also act out of feelings of guilt. Life is busy, and our harried existence rushes us through parenting that may need more of our time. To compensate, who among us hasn't made a quick stop at the toy store or agreed to purchase an outfit that went against our better judgment and our budget?

The fact is, most of us give our daughters too much. The clamor for material possessions that is so prevalent in our society, a clamor encouraged by massive national ad campaigns, creates a kind of static in the environment. Our daughters can't receive a clear signal about what has lasting meaning when there is such a frenzy to consume. Furthermore, the distraction of acquiring more and more distorts a girl's sense of self. According to the Maryland-based Center for a New American Dream, an anticonsumerism organization, "Two-thirds of parents say their kids define their self-worth in terms of possessions."[121]

Ironically, at the same time that we overprovide our children with things, I wonder if we also underprovide them with opportunities to learn from us—mothers, fathers, and teachers—who are dealing every day with whatever our lot in life may be? Brown University President Ruth Simmons has described her childhood in a sharecropper community where her mother, in addition to caring for twelve children, added to the family income by working as a maid and taking in ironing. "When I watched my mother iron those mounds of clothes," she writes, ". . . absolutely insisting that she do the very best job she could, that is how I learned to be a college president. You can teach a child to be a person of quality by showing them how you care for human beings, how you attend to your work, by showing them the standards you set for yourself. That is how you teach children."[122]

Some of the best work we can do together as teachers and parents is to resist the temptation to satisfy all of girls' needs or to cave in to their anger, crankiness, and whining (strategies used more often with parents than with teachers). In addition, we must allow girls to grapple not only with quadratic equations but also with life's steady supply of difficulties. We can be sympathetic and good listeners, but we must not solve their problems. Finally, we should remember that we are giving our daughters everything they really need in life if they know that we struggle to lead lives of discipline and compassion.

Tips & Tactics

Find time to go over the family budget with your daughter. Simplify it so she's not overwhelmed, but by letting her in on the decisions you make routinely about how you earn, spend, and save money, you let her know that you trust her and that she has the maturity to learn some invaluable life lessons.

• • •

Ask your daughter to imagine that she earned a million dollars on her summer vacation and that she must decide how it could be used to improve the lives of others. What would she do with that much money? Build a community center that provides after-school activities for teens? Start a business that employs people who have lost their jobs? This type of activity helps her focus outward, envision herself as someone who can make a difference, and think about what matters most.

27. School Clothes and Life
The Hard Work of Parenting

Clothes were important when I was a teen, but teen fashion wasn't the kazillion-dollar industry it is today. One big difference between forty years ago and now is that there just wasn't as much stuff available. Coming up with the right look didn't require sorting through the piles of choices girls have today. White shirtwaists, straight skirts, black flats, and dyed-to-match outfits for dressier affairs got you through a school year. Back-to-school shopping for Mom and me was relatively simple: do a quick spin through the teen department at Ramsey's or Newman's and then head to the fabric store. I had mostly homemade clothes, which worked well because Mom knew how to add a little extra fabric here and there to accommodate the nonstandard features of my developing body.

By the time my girls were teens, choosing a brand of clothing was a big factor in the fashion-purchase equation. I don't remember any traumatic encounters with my daughters. As long as we were buying Esprit, Benetton, or Lacoste, we had fairly hassle-free shopping excursions. Today, many parents (primarily moms) would rather have a root canal or a flooded basement than a shopping date with their teen.

The hyped-up focus on fashion, the relentless pressure to buy only what's in, and the endless array of choices have created such a frenzy around choosing a wardrobe that some parents are opting out of the mayhem. According to *USA Today*, a "small but burgeoning movement" of parents is hiring personal shoppers.[123] The goal of these parents is not just to manage the trip to the mall but to manage their "limits-pushing daughters" as well.[124]

Teens are more demanding today than we were at their age, but we are often more sensitive and less objective as parents than we need to be. No one wants to have an emotional breakdown with a sobbing teenager in the middle of the juniors section of Macy's, but before we hire an "expert" to mediate skirt length and cleavage, let's make sure we understand what we're trying to avoid.

One parent quoted in the *USA Today* article said, "It would have hurt her feelings if I'd said one thing about something not looking good on her."[125] It is very easy for parents, especially moms, to overidentify with their daughters' disappointments. We quickly put ourselves in our daughters' shoes, recall unhappy times when we were their age, and decide to avoid the situation. But facing disappointment and not always getting one's way are part of living. Girls need to learn how to handle setbacks.

Sometimes our difficulty with teen children is rooted in our own feelings of weakness. I remember backing away from potentially volatile encounters with my daughters because I doubted my ability to stand up to teenage tirades. Wise counsel from a trusted advisor, however, allowed me to see that my lack of confidence was putting my daughters at risk. Teens need us to hold them to certain basic standards of civility. We can't avoid our own personal growth if we seek to be good parents.

It is important to develop the skills to deal effectively with adolescents who desperately want and need to be treated like the young adults they are trying to become. Resolving conflict with a frustrated teen requires us to know something about listening (and hearing even what is not being said), clarifying perceptions, validating our daughters' authority without caving in to unreasonable demands, and generating options. There are few shortcuts. We can't avoid the hard work or the time it takes.

Tips & Tactics

The next time the conversation with your daughter starts to heat up, suggest that she write down her main points in a letter to you. Some girls are more thoughtful and articulate in writing than in one-on-one encounters in the heat of the moment. You may decide to answer her in writing, or better yet, perhaps you can sit down together and review the points she has made.

•••

Set rules of engagement with your daughter. In a calm moment, suggest that you agree on some rules for having the heated conversations that pop up. For example, prefacing a sentence with "I need you to know . . ." provides a more constructive frame for issues she needs to raise with you. For example, "I need you to know that . . .

> . . . sometimes I feel overwhelmed with everything I have to do."

> . . . I feel left out at school."

> . . . I hate being fat."

> . . . I am always anxious about my grades."

Those conversation starters can open the door to a discussion that provides you with the opportunity to acknowledge how your daughter feels and to ask her questions that will allow her to sort out her thoughts:

"Can you tell me more about that?"

"It is really hard to feel that way. Have you talked with anyone else about this?"

"I can hear how upsetting this is. Have you thought about what you could do to make things better?"

28. A Special Case
Refining Our Focus on Our Daughters

In the pre-air-conditioned, pre-TV (in our house) fifties when I was growing up, it was a regular occurrence on hot summer evenings for the phone to ring—there was going to be a hamburger fry at McClelland Park. I loved the picnics and getting together with our friends, but I didn't like McClelland Park. There were no swings or slides; there was nothing for kids to do. It would never have occurred to my folks to take that into consideration when planning these get-togethers. Everyday life all those years ago was organized around adults, not children. Routines and schedules were largely arranged to suit grown-ups; children were on the periphery. So while the hamburgers fried and my parents and their friends stood around and talked without a thought of entertaining us, my brother, the rest of the kids, and I filled the time by collecting discarded bottle caps or scuffing through the gravel around the picnic tables, hoping to find a few coins that had fallen out of pockets.

Along with not being the main attractions, my brother and I also were not burdened with hearing that we were "special." Mom and Dad commended us when we deserved it (making good grades or helping our grandparents), but there were plenty of shape-up lectures, reminding us that we were, if not ordinary, certainly not at risk of being exceptional.

We were cherished and cared for, but according to psychologist Polly Young-Eisendrath, we were lucky to have parents who did not put us at the center of the universe or shower us with excessive praise. In *The Self-Esteem Trap: Raising Confident and Compassionate Kids in an Age of Self-Importance*, she says that "overfocus on the talents, skills, or insights of an individual child (no matter how gifted) naturally leads to an exaggerated self-importance in adolescence and young adulthood" and that this inflated sense of self results in children becoming "preoccupied with their own needs" and feeling entitled.[126]

Many of us from the baby-boom generation, believing we should have had more attention and been noticed more for our uniqueness when we were growing up, set about to correct the deficits. Young-Eisendrath writes, "We gathered in groups large (rock concerts) and small (consciousness-raising) to bring to ourselves the . . . love we collectively longed for . . . [and] eventually . . . dubbed our problem low self-esteem."[127] What is most interesting, however, is how my generation used that frame of reference to shift the paradigm for parenting our own children. Losing sight of the requirement that a child's self-esteem must be grounded in genuinely earned achievement as well as in an understanding and acceptance of her weaknesses, we have gone overboard in praising our offspring and in refusing to let them experience setbacks. We also have allowed our daughters' every whim and desire to dictate how we live our lives. The result is that by the time our offspring are teens and young adults, they may sincerely believe that they *are* special and that the world owes them something. Much that I read about postboomer adults, furthermore, suggests that the next generation of parents is following our example of overpraising children and that they, too, have adopted the role of offspring concierge.

This sense of entitlement is carried through to college classrooms across the country. In a *New York Times* article reporting on college students' expectations for grades, a professor at the University of Maryland is quoted as saying that the grade for meeting the standard course requirements in his classes is a C.[128] He adds, however, that his students "see the default grade as an A."[129] A University of California at Irvine survey cited in the same article also found that a third of students expect a B just for showing up for lectures.[130]

The students' value of effort over mastery is clear. Students commented that "putting in a lot of effort should merit a high grade" and that "what else is there really than the effort you put in?"[131] Students also tend to blame others for poor marks. According to one professor quoted in the article, "Attributing the outcome of a failure to someone else is a common problem."[132]

These attitudes do not bode well for smooth transitions from adolescence into adulthood. No one wants a doctor, veterinarian, attorney, or airline pilot whose focus is on effort instead of end results and who blames others for poor outcomes. Those of our young people who believe that advancement is an unearned privilege and that just showing up is sufficient have a lot to learn before they will be ready to assume adult roles.

At Miss Hall's School, we are committed to preparing girls for future success as well as for inevitable difficulties. We create a structured environment that requires them to take responsibility for their learning, their lives, and their recovery when results aren't what they expect. At home, parents, too, can resist the urge to rescue a daughter when she is disgruntled with outcomes or to join her in blaming others for her shortfalls. The key is to have a girl look inward and find within herself the courage to persist and the capacity to effect the change she wants to see in her life. Sometimes, it is good to look back to the common sense of the old ways.

Tips & Tactics

At the start of a new school year, sport season, or special project, ask your daughter what outcome she hopes to experience. Having her project herself forward will help her think about her goals. Once she has an idea of where she wants to go, suggest that she jot down some ideas about what she will do to prepare for the success she has envisioned.

• • •

Propose that your daughter write down the questions for which she wants answers and what her ideal answer would be. Then ask her to describe the one action she might take that will result in her getting the answer she is looking for, as in the following example:

Question: "Will I be accepted to college?"

Ideal Answer: "One of my top-three colleges accepted me!"

Action: "I will set time aside every weekend to study so I can raise my grades."

29. You're the Top
Honest Responses to Achievement

I couldn't wait to get out to my playhouse, an old chicken coop, on Saturday mornings when I was a kid. My friend Nancy would come over, and we'd begin to list the choices. Would the playhouse be a store today? A New York apartment? A school? Once the decision was made, we'd get to work, using whatever was available: orange crates, cardboard boxes, discarded sheets and draperies, old clothes. It took us hours to get everything right. Apartments took the longest; they needed TVs—a hole cut in a box and a page from a magazine taped across the opening—as well as furniture and appliances. When we finished or got bored with the playhouse, we'd go inside and play jacks. Along toward evening, we'd go back out, find a few more kids, and play tag.

My parents didn't offer incentives for me to entertain myself, and they didn't involve themselves in my play. To be fair, Mom did paint the chicken coup—once—after the chickens moved out. My parents, however, didn't stand in the backyard and applaud when I played store or apartment or tag. They had other things to do—house repairs, laundry, food shopping.

Author Christie Mellor says that today's parents are using "tiny trophies" to bribe their kids "to play a game . . . that in other, simpler times, kids would race out of doors to play all by themselves."[133] She cites as an example the awards five-year-olds get for playing T-ball. Do children receive them because they have shown "particular prowess . . . or . . . fine sportsmanship?" she asks.[134] No, she says, it's just for "showing up."[135]

If we're not careful, we can fall easily into the empty-praise rut, and it's our daughters who suffer when we do. We don't intend to cause harm; we just worry that if we don't applaud everything, girls will feel like failures, their egos will be damaged, or they won't like us anymore. We can stop worrying. As Mellor says, "Children need to earn their self-esteem, not be handed it on a platter."[136]

When we are committed to making our daughters feel good about themselves at all times, we are committed to protecting them from failure. As a result, they lower their sights. In addition, if they never experience disappointment, they are not prepared for it when it arrives. Is it any wonder that we read stories about high-school seniors in a state of emotional collapse when they receive deferral or denial letters from colleges? They have had very little practice with letdown and even less practice coping with it successfully.

I recently spoke with the chair of the science department here at Miss Hall's School about the ninth-grade science fair. As I knew, she understands the problem. Because I had been away at the time of the fair, I asked how it had gone. "Fine," she told me, "but some exhibits, of course, were better than others." Then she added, "And they were graded accordingly."

It is essential that we be honest with girls about their performance. Noted child psychologist and author Michael Riera says that when we overpraise, we encourage the abandonment of self in young people.[137] Kids know when they have not done a good job or their best work. When we swoop in with praise for mediocre effort, they are confused: should they trust their gut feeling or what Mom or Dad is saying? If this adult response continues, girls come to lose confidence in their inner voice, which eventually leaves them susceptible to peer pressure.[138]

As parents, we can't control the world our daughters will inhabit. Ahead of them lie days when their best won't be good enough; when the promotion will go to someone else; or when they will be criticized, teased, or rejected. What we can control, however, is how we prepare girls for the future by encouraging them to reach ever higher toward their goals, to accept failure as a necessary step toward success, and to believe that the best praise they can receive is that which they give themselves for a job well done.

Tips & Tactics

Be careful how you respond to your daughter's failure. Rushing to her defense and joining with her in blaming others enable her to deflect taking responsibility. Even when you believe she has been treated unjustly, it is best to acknowledge that calmly and then ask her how she plans to resolve the issue. What your daughter will glean when you rush in to rescue her is that she can't handle it herself and that you agree she is unable to resolve the issue alone.

•••

Check yourself from time to time to make certain that you have not hitched your own self-esteem as a parent to your daughter's performance in school, on the athletic field, or as a candidate for college. She needs to be free to fail without thinking that you will suffer as a result.

30. Never Home Alone
Allowing Our Daughters to Become Adults

At eighteen, I left home. I went to college, married young, and never moved back into my parents' house. Along the way, my folks contributed good advice (when to rotate tires or call the plumber), reassurance (through my daughters' temper tantrums), and a loan (when it was time to buy a house), but they basically led their lives and let me lead mine.

With my daughters, it was a different story. When they were eighteen, I was just beginning to entertain the idea that they might possibly be able to drive alone on the Beltway in Washington, DC, and ride the Metro without me. Although this is a slight exaggeration, it is a fact that my and my husband's involvement in our children's lives (we have four adult children between us) throughout their late teens and twenties has been considerably greater than what we experienced with our own parents.

Evidently, we are typical of our generation. As a cohort of parents, baby boomers have turned parenting into a long career. Fortunately, our four offspring are on their own and are self-sufficient, but many people our age are finding themselves looking after adult children who still turn to their parents for everything from food to fulfillment. Social psychologist

Jane Adams, author of *When Our Grown Kids Disappoint Us: Letting Go of Their Problems, Loving Them Anyway, and Getting on with Our Lives*, says, "Despite having every constitutional and environmental advantage . . . many of our children are not growing into the independent, generous, kind, happy, successful, law-abiding, contributing citizens we expected them to be."[139] In extreme cases, parents spend retirement dollars to bail irresponsible kids out of credit-card debt or remortgage their homes to address their kids' substance abuse, which surveys show is on the rise in middle-class young adults.[140] Most disconcerting is that young adults with potential are seriously stalled in becoming productive members of society.

So, what went wrong? How could the children of the "largest, richest, and most educated generation in history" be on such a long runway to responsible adulthood?[141] Adams says that the emphasis on happiness that emerged during the Me Decade of the seventies is partially to blame. "With parents having gone to sometimes extraordinary lengths to ensure their kids' happiness," she writes, "it's no surprise that their grown children expect them to continue to provide it."[142] In our attempt to keep our offspring smiling, we have taught them that happiness is *their* right and *our* responsibility, and they cling to that idea long after it's in their best interest not to do so.

Most parents would agree that keeping an eye on what is in the long-term best interest of our children is the priority when making parenting decisions. The challenge for those just beginning to parent adolescents is to do that amid the competing interests, distractions, and pressures in today's society. The fact is that if we want our daughters to be ready to embrace all the opportunities that lie ahead, as well as to assume responsibility for their lives and their happiness, we will make the necessary adjustments to our parenting techniques now, during their teen years.

One of those adjustments is to see the budding young woman peeking out from under the brim of the baseball cap. William Aquilino, a noted authority in the field of emerging adulthood, says that "critical tasks facing parents and their offspring during [this phase] include parental acknowledgement of the *adult status* of their child."[143] Although our teens are not yet adults, it is not too early to insist that they grapple with such adult issues as accountability, consequences, and inconvenience. When we allow them to struggle as well as to feel the joy of succeeding, we have, in fact, allowed them to create their own happiness. Spending time teaching our children this now will go a long way toward ensuring our own happiness in retirement.

Tips & Tactics

The locus of control for your daughter's life must be within her, not with her peer group. Take note when she is looking to others to tell her what to do and say. To encourage her to make her own decisions, be ready with statements or questions that ask her to reflect on what she wants, thinks, and believes:

"I'd be interested in your opinions."

"What do you think?"

"Why is this important to you?"

"What do you think matters most now?"

Even when you can't agree with your daughter's opinions, confirm the value of her expressing them with a comment such as "Interesting insight" or "What a unique idea."

31. That's Life!
Weathering Trials and Triumphs

I competed for my share of prizes and positions when I was young. I entered the Independent Grocers' Association spelling bee and won a half-gallon of ice cream (third prize). I submitted artwork to the Clean-Up, Fix-Up, Paint-Up poster contest in my hometown and won something, but I can't remember what. Then I auditioned to be *the* school musical accompanist and landed that position. But when I tried out for drum majorette with Top Hatters, the high-school drum and bugle corps, I was passed over and had to settle for bugle sergeant.

When events went my way, Mom and Dad said, "Good for you!" When they didn't, I always heard some version of "That's life! You can't have the sunny days without the rainy ones. Better luck next time." My parents viewed the normal ups and downs of growing up as routine. My failure to carry the big baton in marches on Main Street didn't send my parents into a depression. Not so with many parents today.

On the whole, today's parents not only overmanage their children but overidentify with their offspring's success—or lack thereof. Research says that when little Emmy isn't chosen for the lead in the play, it is the parent's emotional health that suffers most. A growing segment of today's parents measure their self-worth by their children's achievements and have worse mental health than parents who have learned to step back and engage less emotionally.[144]

The backdrop for this phenomenon is the hypercompetitive nature of our society. For some reason we have the idea that we, our children, our house, our car, and our pets are all in some kind of huge competition and that we are useless if we don't win out over everyone else, in everything, every time. According to journalist Sue Shellenbarger, we know the stress that getting into the "right" college creates for teens, but we have also learned that many parents believe that the arrival of the thick envelope of college acceptance will confirm not only their daughter's place in the entering class but their own social standing and worth as parents.[145] If the thin envelope of admission rejection arrives instead, parents are consumed with guilt and anxiety.

According to the research, overinvolved parents also don't feel joyful or content when their children actually do win the election or graduate at the top of the class.[146] Even in these circumstances, overinvolved moms and dads scored low on tests that measured mental health. Study coauthor Missa Murry Eaton says, according to Shellenbarger, that apparently "the ever-present threat of a child's failure looms so large that it blots out any joy over the successes."[147]

Girls are always aware when parents have become inappropriately tangled in their lives. Whether our misguided involvement takes the shape of overprotecting, over-problem-solving, overpraising, overempathizing, or being overdependent on our daughters' triumphs to validate who we are, the result is the same: our daughters can't break free to develop into competent and self-reliant young women. Furthermore, we have missed an opportunity to model the individuated life, the life that is contained and authentic.

Preparing for college and life is hard work. The threads of responsibility, challenge, exhilaration, discovery, and disappointment are all woven together into the fabric of a girl's days. There will be good times and bad; friends will be true and fickle; homesickness will recede only to make a surprise reappearance; games will be won and lost; understanding will dissolve into confusion. As my parents told me, that's life. The important thing to remember is that your daughter's successes and shortfalls are not about you. Her life journey is uniquely her own. We will be tempted to rush onto a girl's path when she stubs her toe or takes a fall, but we must resist the urge. She will regain her balance, and if we just let her, so may we.

Tips & Tactics

Listen for the first-person plural pronoun *we* when you are talking about your daughter. If you say, for example, "We are applying to college this fall" or "We are hoping to be editor of the school paper," that is a dead giveaway that you are too enmeshed with your daughter's life.

•••

Examine your feelings the next time your daughter is passed over for the lead part in the play or receives a rejection letter from her number-one college choice. Is your disappointment centered in empathy for her? Or are you worried about losing face with your friends? Has your pride in being a parent suffered a blow?

32. Beyond the Stars
Finding the College That Fits

One of the difficult realities of school life today is the numbers game of college admission. I call it a numbers game, though we know it is more than that. The process of getting into college has been transformed in recent years by the increasingly high number of applications that colleges receive annually. There was a time when the most selective colleges, for example, accepted 20 percent of applicants, and we thought that was rough. Today many colleges accept fewer than 13 percent, with Ivy League schools often accepting in the single digits.

There are more students than ever before applying to college. Students, parents, and schools are aware of this, so students increase the number of applications they submit in order to improve their chances of acceptance to at least one of their top choices. In addition, each student wants what she perceives to be an advantage in the job market and thus applies to and sets her heart on the big-name colleges. The result is college application inflation and a sort of college star system.

These phenomena are familiar to us from other contexts. The stock market is carried by tremendous investment in a few stocks and little or not enough in most. A few athletes make millions of dollars, while the majority make very little. Barnes and Noble primarily promotes books by star authors. And on and on.

Most of us, though, are not part of the star system. What we try to do in our lives is to learn and grow, to make a contribution to society, to stay connected with other people, and to do things that have deep and lasting value. If, when we do that, we also make it onto the cover of *Time* magazine, become CEO of Disney, win the Olympic gold—or gain acceptance into all twelve colleges of our choice—well, that is good, but it is not the essence of who we are. The essence is that we know how to do good things in all of life's circumstances.

Spring is the season of triumph and despair for seniors. One day there is the elation of that magical acceptance letter, and with the next day comes the dumbstruck disappointment of the rejection from the college that the girl knew absolutely for certain would take her. I am not saying that success does not matter, or that all colleges are the same. They are not. But of the several thousand colleges in the United States, a very large number are motivated by the same basic values that motivate all of us as educators. They offer excellent programs taught by devoted professors, and the degrees they bestow will help students begin their careers. Quality in American higher education is spread broadly; it is not concentrated at the top.

What seems more important than being accepted into the "right" college is finding the college that fits. If each student's list of colleges comprises excellent institutions that fit her ambitions, talents, and preferences, then, in the end, she will make a choice in a sober, not a star-struck, frame of mind.

As I watch students manage the stress of the college admission process, I often think, just wait until you are parents. You will go through it all again, vicariously, and it is likely to be even more stressful! We all, and I most definitely include myself, painfully identify with our children as they are about to leave home. We want everything to be perfect for them, and we can have a pretty narrow idea of what perfect means. The result, in my case, was that I forgot to trust what I had already taught my daughters. I forgot to trust that they were good and competent people who could not only make the decision about where to apply to college but do well wherever they ended up.

The fact is that the college race is only a small part of a large life. Ultimately, what an adolescent girl has learned from parents and school and what she brings with her deep in her spirit will take over and make her life one of purpose and value to herself and to others.

Tips & Tactics

Girls benefit when we teach them how to think about their futures with some broad goals in mind. College admission, for example, should be about a step toward something, rather than an end in itself. A Passion and Talent List might help your daughter begin to identify where her life path might be leading. Suggest that she make two lists, one labeled "I am passionate about . . ." and the second labeled "I know I'm really good at . . . ." Where does she see a connection between her true passions and her true strengths?

33. Eyes on the Prize
Stepping Back from Adolescent Difficulties

An alumna tells the story of approaching Miss Hall's School's founder, Mira Hall, in a panic. "May I quickly send a telegram to Father?" she asked. "Is something wrong, dear?" Miss Hall replied. "Oh, yes," said the alumna, "I have forgotten Father's birthday." Suffice it to say that what was a crisis for the alumna as an adolescent was not a crisis for our first headmistress. Permission was denied on the basis that the alumna should have planned better, and the alumna was sent to write a note, undoubtedly with an apology explaining her tardiness. The lesson was not lost on this girl. "I was really upset with Miss Hall at the time," she told me recently, "but it never happened again."

Mira Hall was a wise educator of girls, and stories like this prove it. Not overly concerned about the frustration this student was experiencing, she did not make it her job to eliminate the immediate problem. Rather, she had her eyes on a larger goal, one that had to do with developing a girl's responsibility and accountability. I suspect that for Miss Hall, letting a teenager suffer through the pain of knowing she had possibly disappointed a parent was a small price for the prize of a girl's learning to plan ahead.

There *is* a greater goal than eliminating difficulty instantly. Adolescents can't see down the road to what life is likely to require of them. That's our job as educators and as parents. If we jump in to solve girls' problems, we lose sight of what's important in the long run and actually give the problems more weight and standing than they should have. Girls want us to listen, to be sensitive to their feelings, but not to have the same meltdown reaction to difficulty that they experience. Adult meltdown is frightening to them. When they call home to tell us the sky is falling, they need us to say, "No, it's not." Then they can calm down and solve the problem.

This is easier said than done. Every parent, even the most clear thinking, can get sucked into overinvolvement when it comes to a daughter. After all, our protective instincts were required when she was a baby and a toddler. But just as our daughters grow up and move beyond the fenced-in backyard, we must grow with them and provide what they most need now. Overprotecting keeps them childlike and dependent, exactly the opposite of what we want for them. When we have the courage (and courage is what it takes) to insist that their problems remain their problems, not ours, girls can keep moving toward the bigger goal of self-reliance.

For example, returning to school after vacation is exciting, but it is also a time of uncertainty. Whether a girl is returning to the same school or changing schools, she is making a new start, reuniting with friends, making new friends, joining a new team, or being presented with higher academic expectations. This kind of change is bound to bring some temporary frustration. It is normal, then, for adolescents to expect, even to demand, immediate solutions.

Unfortunately, we have taught them to respond that way as our society has become increasingly more child oriented. A century ago, our offspring were short adults, working alongside us to keep the farm, family business, or household running. Today, we know that children need to be cared for, nurtured, and educated. We have eliminated from their lives most, if not all, of their meaningful contributions to family life and a lot of the struggle that goes with it. I'm not suggesting we roll back child-labor laws and serve skimpy portions of gruel in dimly lit kitchens. But our child-centered child rearing has inadvertently placed children in a sort of Camelot world where all of life's problems, like Camelot's leaves, fall into neat little piles that we parents end up toting away.

There are variations, of course, in girls' abilities to cope. Some girls arrive with more "success connectors" than others. When difficulty arrives, some girls can think, I've been here before. I remember what I did. I remember what didn't work. I know what to do now. Other girls have not had that experience. For them, the opening of a new school year will bring great challenge. As psychologist William Damon writes in *Greater Expectations: Overcoming the Culture of Indulgence in Our Homes and Schools*, children need "a framework of adult guidance in the face of life's complexities [but] not a protective bubble that shields out reality."[148]

Damon quotes from Joseph Conrad's short story "Youth," which is about a young man (imagine it's a young woman) on a ship. The young man faced every hardship imaginable, from storms, squalor, and rats to an explosion on board that left him alone on the high seas in a lifeboat. Looking back on the adventure from middle age, the sailor says, "There was also my youth to make me patient . . . wasn't that the best time, that time when we were young at sea . . . on the sea that gives nothing except hard knocks—and sometimes a chance to feel your strength."[149]

Girls need to grapple with difficulty, to work out their own solutions, to develop patience for the process, and to feel their own strengths. When your daughter has problems, you don't need to solve them for her, worry about her unhappiness, or feel guilty about letting her struggle. Listen, be sympathetic, and guide her work with your questions: "What have you tried so far? What is your next step? Where will you go for assistance?" But most of all, keep your eyes on the prize: a resilient and competent young woman in a few short years. And if we hear that your daughter has forgotten your birthday, we're going to suggest egreetings.com.

Tips & Tactics

When your daughter has a problem, listen, be sympathetic, and guide with your questions. Here are a few to keep handy the next time there is a problem:

"What do you think you should do first about this?"

"What have you tried so far?"

"What is your next step?"

"Who is your best advisor for this issue?"

"Is there anything you have done before in solving a similar problem that you think could work here?"

34. Our Strongest, Best Selves
What We Learn from Our Daughters

When someone comments on an idea that I have put forth about adolescent girls, I am always reminded that parenting was my crash course, not only in learning how to deal with teenagers, but also in building confidence—my own. I was undaunted by job pressures, solo piano recitals, and eighteen-hour workdays, but my two teenage daughters were a different story. It is to my daughters that I attribute much of my growing up. Whatever deficits in confidence and self-esteem I brought to adulthood were addressed through parenting.

It is only recently that we as a society have realized how important it is for each girl to find her voice. This is a polite way of saying that rebellious sass wasn't acceptable when I was growing up, not that I didn't try it. Any spurts of back talk I initiated were short lived. My parents weren't having it.

Somewhere between the early sixties, when I was a teenager, and the early nineties, when my girls were in their teens, the rules changed, but I must not have been at the meeting. My daughters were much less inhibited as teenagers than I was, and I found myself standing in front of in-your-face adolescents who had an uncanny ability to discover my most vulnerable sides. During those years, I went into survival mode and read every book I could find on growing teens, consulted with my parents, and finally had a long talk with myself about what I would and would not accept from someone not even close to half my age.

Because my girls insisted that I be a stronger adult, I assumed that this is what all kids do for all parents. Then recently, while having lunch with a group of alumnae in Florida, the discussion about parenting differences among generations came up, as it usually does with women who are of my generation or older. At some point in the conversation, an alumna in her sixties sitting across the table from me said, "I don't think I taught my parents anything." Her comment stopped me in my tracks. What a thought! I could not wait to call my parents.

The next morning, I phoned Missouri. "Did my brother and I teach you guys anything?" I asked. The first clue that I might be onto something came when my mom said, "I never really thought about it." "Never thought about it? Don't you know?" I asked, incredulous.

While my mother was beginning to consider my question, my dad, on the other phone, added with his typical humor, "Sure, you taught me something—that parents inherit gray hair from their kids." I chuckled. "And I learned to pray more often, every time you drove off with the car." Very funny.

By now my mother was ready to contribute the thought that I *had* taught her some things, but she wasn't sure what they were. Having tried out all of his jokes, Dad calmed down and admitted that my brother and I had increased his patience and understanding. Well, that's something, I thought.

The next phone calls were to my two daughters. Did they know the impact they had made on me? I woke up my twenty-six-year-old on a Sunday morning. "Do you think you taught me anything?" I asked. "I don't mean which scarf to wear with which suit, I mean . . ." "I know, Mom," she interrupted. "You mean like how to be a better person." Still sounding groggy, she said simply, "Yes," and added, "I'll call you later when I wake up."

Daughter number two was not out of bed but at least was awake when I called, so the conversation had a bit more flow. "Oh, good grief. You always ask these cheesy questions," she said. To my total surprise, she had to think about her response and at first said, "I don't know." How on earth was it possible that she and I could have argued as we had and she not think I had grown stronger as a result? Within a few minutes, however, she was willing to concede that "we were constantly learning from each other." An understatement if I ever heard one.

I raised the topic again at another lunch with a different group of alumnae a few days later. These were all women who had graduated from Miss Hall's School prior to 1942. I asked if they thought they had taught their parents anything. "If I did, they never would have admitted it," one woman quickly responded. Another added, "I doubt it, because they really weren't listening to me." The conversation continued with each of us thinking about the topic from the point of view of ourselves both as mothers and as daughters, with so many opinions and variations in the responses around the table that I came away believing that the whole issue would make a great research project.

The irony of my experience with my daughters is that adolescents do not decide to be difficult to help their parents become more confident adults. Since the sixties, it has been the well-recognized job of teenagers to elbow at their limitations, assert a developing self, demand to be heard, and try to control. Not all confrontation from our adolescent daughters is cranky stubbornness. Out of the mouths of babes and teenagers sometimes comes wisdom we should listen to.

Regardless of how much we believe that each generation learns from or teaches the next, two important thoughts emerge from these discussions. First, we have a moral responsibility to be our strongest, best selves and to insist that our daughters be the same. And second, being our best requires courage in the face of difficulty, open-mindedness to change, and an indomitable spirit. At least that's what it took for me to convince my daughters and myself that I was still in charge.

Tips & Tactics

Allowing abusive behavior from a teen to go unchecked teaches her that she can have her way by mistreating others. When the attacks are flying, model the behavior your daughter needs to see. Stay calm, but be firm and direct when you say something like the following:

"Those comments are hurtful."

"I cannot allow you to be rude and disrespectful to me."

"Let's continue this when we have both calmed down."

35. Lighten Up
Worried Parenting

It was a little before 1:00 a.m. one hot August night in pre-air-conditioned Missouri, and my boyfriend, his mother, and I were sitting on the front porch of his house trying to stay cool. Suddenly a car pulled up, and through the still night air, I heard my father say, "Jeannie, get yourself home!" I was shocked! I had never had a curfew, and I guess I had never stayed out late enough for my parents to be concerned before, but on that night they were Worried.

How much time do we spend as parents worrying about our children? In his book *Worried All the Time: Overparenting in an Age of Anxiety and How to Stop It*, psychologist David Anderegg says, "We do worry more than parents used to worry, and we worry more than we need to."[150] I don't need to see that in print to know it's true. I admit that I worry about my twenty-something daughters. When the phone rings, I'm sure there is some calamity. When the phone doesn't ring, I wonder why they're not calling. Throughout my daughters' teenage years, I worried, as you do, about everything from drugs, sex, and hip-hop to violence in movies to air pollution. We can all agree that there are more roads to trouble now than there were in the Pleasantville fifties. But that is not the only reason worry too often consumes us.

Family size contributes to our overanxiousness. We have smaller families today, which means that the anxiety most of us experience over our first-born child never has a chance to dissipate over four or five children. Anderegg says, "The kind of placidity and blissful nonchalance that characterizes the parenting of younger children in a large family is rapidly becoming a forgotten memory."[151] We also don't live in the shelter of an extended family as we used to, where grandparents and even great-grandparents could calm our nerves and give us the reassurance that only age and experience can give.

Maybe we read too much. With an overabundance of books on parenting available, we can't possibly understand and do everything that is recommended. We also try to take charge too often when we're parenting our daughters, which is guaranteed to leave us in a fretful stew. The more we pull one way, the more the teenager must pull in the other. The result is often a high-pitched confrontation leaving us feeling out of control and . . . worried.

At the start of a new school year, there is no shortage of things to worry about for parents of teenage girls. Will my daughter make friends? Do well academically? Make the team? Handle difficulty? Steer clear of alcohol and drugs? I offer a few suggestions on how we can keep our balance:

Listen when your daughter is upset, but don't allow her to transfer her misery onto you. Girls are experts at this, particularly with moms.

Try not to transfer your anxiety about your daughter onto her. She will interpret your worry as lack of confidence in her ability to manage difficulty.

Resist the need to let your own negative experiences as a teenager trigger a response in you. Your daughter needs your best listening ear when she is feeling lonely and left out, not the emotional reaction of a parent who remembers a similar slight.

Respond to your daughter's setbacks with as much relaxed composure as you can summon. When my daughters are anxious, I have found that my calm voice (even if it's simulated) at the other end of the phone is the most helpful.

Checking in too frequently with your daughter not only raises her anxiety level but yours as well. If your daughter is away at school, agree to e-mail or talk on the phone two to three times a week (instead of two to three times a day), and you both will benefit from a more ordered approach to each other.

If your daughter is at home during the high-school years, you may begin to feel that she sometimes moves away emotionally. Do not despair. Girls have serious work to do between the ages of fourteen and eighteen, figuring out who they are and learning to stand on their own. Some girls stay connected through this phase, and some girls need more distance. Give her the space she needs, but let her know you are there if she needs to talk.

Say to yourself as often as needed, lighten up Girls are actually more resilient than we think. If we keep our emotional balance, they will amaze us with their resourcefulness.

I would suggest, however, that you set a curfew. It will save you a lot of worry and your daughter a lot of embarrassment.

Tips & Tactics

Staying connected to our daughters but detaching emotionally from them during the teen years is the goal for parents. It is a difficult skill to learn, and it can be helpful for you to have a coach (spouse, friend, or older family member) who is not emotionally connected to your daughter and who can help you maintain perspective.

36. Yielding Control
Encouraging Growth by Letting Go

There are some things girls can learn only if we, as parents, get out of the way. I am reminded of telephone conversations that often play out between parents and their boarding-school or college daughters. If you're like me, you get these calls on the one night you have finally gotten to bed at a reasonable hour, so you're well into the first sleep stage when you hear your daughter's voice. "This is all a huge mistake. I want to come home," she sobs.

For all but the most savvy and disciplined parents, that call can be a serious temptation to swing into action. When our daughters are scared, it's natural for us to be scared too. Confronting a tearful plea for help, most of us have an immediate reaction to want to rescue our child from the pain she is experiencing. But the fact is that if we rush in to save the day for our adolescent daughters, we make two mistakes.

First, we forget what the real work of the adolescent years is. In addition to learning French, algebra, and Chinese language and culture, girls between the ages of fourteen and eighteen are adapting to their bodies, forming identities and values, understanding intimacy, and making friends. In order to do this work, girls must learn to manage their emotions, time, and relationships, to say nothing of their money and their laundry. In fact, one of the reasons families value the boarding-school experience is that girls can make a gradual transition into taking full responsibility for all these aspects of adult life while still under the watchful eyes of caring adults.

Our second mistake is in getting too involved. A counselor friend once said to me that when we, as parents or teachers, put ourselves in the middle of the issues our adolescent is grappling with, she has to steer around us to get to the solution. In a sense, we block her vision. Teens know that they must separate from their parents and become independent. We only add to their confusion when we keep asserting ourselves where we do not belong.

There is also an added cost to a daughter when we take over instead of letting her be in charge. When we assume responsibility for solving her problems, we prevent her from believing that she is strong and capable. And if she does not feel that sense of competence that comes from solving a problem, she cannot feel confident about herself. In short, we have robbed her of an opportunity to grow. Girls become confident by doing, not merely by being told what they can do.

Staying out of the way does not mean staying out of touch. Our daughters need us as much as they always have, just in a different way. We need to learn to listen more and to restate a daughter's comments nonjudgmentally so she can reflect on what she has said and try to hear the subtext. The tearful "I want to come home" can be translated into "Will I be accepted in this new place?" or "Can I do the academic work here?" "I have no privacy" signals that a girl may not yet have learned how to set boundaries.

We also need to try not to let our emotions mirror those of our daughters. This is tough. If a girl is anxious about making friends, adding our anxiety does not help. If she is in tears over a bad English grade, this is not our cue to remind her of our expectations. The I-want-to-come-home message is not an invitation to jump in the car and make a frantic drive to campus. Her announcement that she didn't make varsity soccer should not give us permission to declare that her college options will be cut in half.

As parents, we have always needed to make adjustments as our children pass through the various stages of childhood. Potty trainer, chauffeur, peacemaker—each role requires a slightly different approach.

However, fine-tuning our skills for the adolescent years may be the hardest adjustment of all. Letting out the last piece of string on the kite is scary, because we are losing our control. But unless we yield that control to our daughters, gradually and over time, they will never learn to manage well in the world. That is what we must remember.

Tips & Tactics

Yielding control is easier when we can remember what is in our daughters' long-term best interests. When a teen is thinking only of short-term solutions, acknowledge her feelings, then ask questions that encourage her to take a longer view:

"I can hear how frustrating this is. What are you thinking you might do now? Do you think there might be someone to help you solve this?"

"I can hear how hurtful it was to be ignored by your friend. Do you think you might be able to tell her how you feel? Do you think there is a way to mend the friendship?"

"I can hear how disappointed you are in not making the team. What are you thinking you might do instead? Does it make sense to try and learn more about what you can do to improve your chances for next season?"

37. A Life of One's Own
Fostering Independence

New York apartment, dress shop, office, school—all located in my backyard playhouse—were the rooms of my imagination, the places I visited to create my world of pretend. Since Mom and Dad rarely showed up there, it was a place where I was free. So fond of this pretend universe was I that when I moved beyond elementary school and outgrew my first imaginary haunts, I still arranged for a semiprivate realm. The relative safety of a small Midwest town in the late fifties and early sixties allowed my girlfriends and me to explore our neighborhoods as well as our emerging independence in private, distanced again from the intrusive gaze of our parents. When we were back in the presence of adults, we had our own lexicon—code words and silly names for each other—that kept our parents from moving too far into our private domain.

In 1959 Iona and Peter Opie wrote *The Lore and Language of Schoolchildren*, based on their classic study that positioned childhood as a discreet land for children only. The Opies collected and studied the games, riddles, rhymes, songs, behaviors, and language of children over a period of several years. In the introduction to the second edition of their work, cultural historian Marina Warner writes that the work "explicitly presupposes that a realm of young people exists, distinct and separate from the adult world."[152] Warner states that it is children's vernacular, their "verbal play," among other factors, that "defines borders" and builds the "scaffolding of social identity . . . [and a] . . . sense of belonging."[153]

This sense of belonging to a discreet group, one that is set apart from the parent, enables the child to take the first steps toward independence. Swiss psychiatrist Carl Jung wrote about the development of a distinct personality demanding "the conscious and unavoidable separation of the single individual" from the "undifferentiated group."[154] For an adolescent girl, this group is her family. It is essential that our daughters clear a space between themselves and us, their parents, so that they can begin to step back from our approval and direction and become their own agents. At a time in our societal evolution when parents are hyperinvolved with teens and electronically tethered 24/7, this is easier said than done.

In a *Wall Street Journal* article, author Sam Schulman has written about the difficulty today's parents have in letting go. "Parental hovering," he says, "has destroyed the private lives of children."[155] Gone are the days, Schulman writes, when "knots of children wandered erratically to their schoolhouse or back home" and could begin to create space between themselves and parents.[156] One only needs to read the newspaper to know that gone also are the days when adolescents simply went off to college and to their private worlds. As any college dean of students will tell you, helicopter parents expend a good bit of effort hovering over offspring in colleges and universities from coast to coast.

Schulman's point, one grounded in developmental psychology, is that this extension of parents' hyperinvolvement is a problem. Myriad interactions with others outside the family are required for a teen to stand on her own. "Hovering parents," he writes, "undermine the influence not only of other institutions like schools and churches but of peers," adding that "the seemingly obvious notion that kids need to be left alone sometimes if they are to grow up has been . . . lost."[157]

During Miss Hall's School's family weekend in October, parents of ninth and tenth graders often say that their daughters call home far less than expected. We reassure them that this is a good thing. Five weeks into the school year, girls are adjusting well, making connections, and opening new conduits for interacting with peers and adults. Whether boarders or day students, they are fully engaged, and as a result, a healthy distance emerges between parents and daughters. From our perspective as educators, girls eagerly begin to experience a bigger world and to enjoy a more mature version of themselves in it.

As we all know, the world isn't as safe as it was when I was a teen. That doesn't mean, however, that a girl's need for more privacy in an expanded community has disappeared. Boarding schools and sleep-away summer camps are adult-rich settings that encourage girls to develop their autonomy. Whether by accessing those settings or by structuring the home environment in a way that nurtures self-sufficiency, we will serve our teen daughters well by providing an environment that is a purposeful midpoint between family and adult independence.

Tips & Tactics

Think about ways that your daughter can safely create distance from you and honor her need to clear a space for herself. Then set the boundaries that will give you reassurance that she can be safe in that space (both virtual and actual). Finally, work with her so she can understand where the boundaries are and what is required of her to honor them.

38. On the Road Again
The Need for Disengagement

I knew as I boarded the van to camp that it would be a week before I'd see Mom and Dad again. With a neatly packed Samsonite suitcase and money for evening canteen and crafts, I was on my way, not anticipating the homesickness that descended about twenty-four hours into life at Camp YoCoMo.

The week that stretched before me might as well have been six months. There were no cell phones (I'm not sure there were any phones), no e-mails or faxes, and in those days, telling anyone you were feeling glum wasn't in style. So I toughed it out and . . . prayed (it was church camp). As a result of divine intervention and/or the absence of any other options, I worked through the loneliness and ended up having a great time. Meanwhile, as far as I knew, my parents were home, going about business as usual, not pining for me.

According to a *New York Times* article, children today may be enjoying their sleep-away camp experiences, but many parents are not. The article quotes one consultant who said that camps are employing full-time parent liaisons to help parents deal with the anxiety over their children's being away at camp.[158] Reading this, I decided to call my mom to check my assumption that she and Dad had not been worried or anxious about my managing without them. "Heavens no!" she said when I asked if she had worried; then she added, "Were we supposed to?"

I realize that I was only away for a week, but I'm pretty sure that my parents wouldn't have felt any differently had camp been a month long. It is not that I was completely forgotten; the care package of LifeSavers (five-flavor rolls) and spearmint gum arrived midweek. But my mother's comment about how she and Dad viewed the experience describes where their focus was: "We knew you would have a good time and learn things." In other words, I needed to move beyond what was familiar and comfortable, and this was what they could provide.

Psychologist and author Mary Pipher has written at length about the role of families. She writes that in addition to family members caring for each other, "families have had two other roles—to protect and to socialize," the latter being about "connecting of children to a larger world of meaning."[159] She adds that these roles "are often at odds with each other," and we see that tension today more clearly than ever before.[160]

News stories abound about hyperagent, superinvolved helicopter parents going to great lengths not only to broaden the horizons of their offspring—athletic, cultural, and educational—but also to stay engaged and to monitor, never being more than a text message or Skype call away. Admittedly, parents today have more to worry about when it comes to protecting children. However, we can all agree that although there are more dangers today, the level of parental vigilance and involvement is usually out of proportion to the level of actual protection our children need.

The truth is that as a generation of parents, we have more difficulty disengaging from our offspring than did our parents or grandparents. As one expert quoted in the *Times* article points out, "Nobody goes to school [to learn] how to send your child away from you."[161] Send away? The very phrase gives most of us a chill. We acknowledge that our goal is for our daughters to become self-reliant and confident young women who can cope successfully with challenges. Stated another way, we acknowledge that we cringe at the thought of a thirty-five-year-old daughter still living under our roof and asking how to plug in the toaster. All that notwithstanding, we find it difficult to accept the fact that our teens need to confront the challenges of developing independence as surely as they need to confront the challenges of learning algebra or how to drive a car.

Skillful parenting, therefore, requires us to understand why we insist on being overly involved with our maturing daughters. Psychologist and author Maryann Rosenthal writes in a popular parenting book that "parents must examine their own lust for control," which can prevent teens from taking responsibility for their own actions.[162] The goal, as Rosenthal explains, is to become skilled at detaching, being able to keep "a bit of a psychological distance."[163] This means "seeing yourself as an *observer*," she adds, rather than as someone "who's elated or wounded by your teen's every minor triumph or small misstep."[164]

When our daughters pack their L.L.Bean duffels, actually or metaphorically, and head out for a new school year, they will connect with ever-expanding worlds of meaning and continue the hard work of growing up. This is a good time for moms and dads to continue their own difficult but rewarding work of detaching so that girls have their parents' full support for becoming the self-sufficient and competent young women they are meant to be.

Tips & Tactics

Examine your need for control when you have the impulse to become overinvolved with your teen daughter.

Do you use the first-person plural pronoun when referring to your daughter's affairs? ("We have a term paper due.")

When your daughter has a setback, do you automatically rush to make everything all right again?

When others (such as teachers, coaches, or supervisors at summer jobs) hold your daughter accountable, do you immediately defend her even before knowing all the facts?

If you could prevent your daughter from ever being disappointed or frustrated by the normal ups and downs of life, would you? If the answer is yes, ask yourself how you would then expect her to learn the skills she needs to cope with disappointment.

When we need our daughters' successes to boost our own self-esteem, when our daughters' missteps make us feel like failures as parents, when our moods rise and fall based on whether or not our daughters are having a good or bad day, we are too identified with them. Reflect on your behaviors to determine if you need to create a healthier connection with your daughter.

39. Less Is More
Giving Girls the Confidence to Succeed

I was surprised by what Mr. Stewart wrote in my copy of *Joplinmo*, my high-school yearbook. He was my junior-year English teacher, and as a literary type, he seemed chiefly interested in the degree to which his students grasped the subtler points of *Moby Dick* and *Leaves of Grass*. Although my parents were many things, they were not littérateurs, and it was a big leap for me to engage in the literary criticism of the day. "Leaves of grass," as far as I knew, were pretty much leaves of grass, and as for the great white whale, I was more concerned with who might want to head to the Dairy Queen after school to get a Dilly Bar.

So when I read Mr. Stewart's words, I was taken aback. I probably expected something like "You do work hard" or "Why not try *Pride and Prejudice?*" But instead, he wrote, "I shall not worry about you, for I know you will always manage."

Always manage? Was that like manage to get through the book, manage to get through the class, or something a little more telling? You will always cope? Always prevail? Always triumph? I decided on the latter. The impact of his comment and how I interpreted it over forty years ago was confirmed when I checked back, just to be certain he had written what I remembered, and was amazed to see "manage," not "triumph."

Recently I heard a young woman, a graduate student at Columbia University's Teachers College, describe a moment several years ago when she was walking past the head of school's office at the all-girls school where she had graduated the spring before. Upon hearing the young alumna's voice in the hall, the head of school came out to greet her. As the young woman described it, at some point in their conversation, "the head made a casual comment and asked me, 'When are you going to take over my job?'" Reflecting on that moment in relation to her decision to seek a career in educational administration, the alumna said, "I guess she knew before I did that I could do this."

It is our job as parents and teachers to know before our daughters and students do that they can reach their goals and then to convey that certainty. Girls must be able to trust that we have complete confidence in their ability to achieve so that they will have the courage to take the healthy risks that lead to success. Our best intentions in this work can become misdirected, however. Here are two ways that we most easily lose focus.

First, in our great eagerness to nurture our daughters' potential, we can oversupport them to the point that we are doing their work for them. We have all read news articles about parents writing and editing college papers for their offspring or providing wake-up calls so their twenty-year-old children won't be late for work. We've also read stories about thirty-year-olds moving back in with their parents because they can't cope with adulthood—an unattractive outcome to our being a constant prop for our children. Our role as parents is to cheer and coach from the sidelines but not to run the ball for them. Doing that deprives them of the opportunity to succeed or to learn from failure.

Second, we miss the mark in championing our daughters' noble work toward shaping purposeful, authentic, and fulfilling lives when we have, as one father of a Miss Hall's School alumna stated, unfair expectations. He wrote to the school recently about his daughter's success at college, and in his e-mail he included some reflections on the most important lesson he had learned about parenting. "Do not make," he wrote, "an inordinate emotional investment in a specific outcome you want for your daughter or son—whether that means the results of the game or the casting of a play or the college the child attends." These expectations, he continued, "distort your view and understanding of your child because they are inevitably based on your image of who the child is and what she ought to become. . . . [They] are really more about something we want for ourselves—and in our focus and obsession, we often fail to see this authentic young woman emerging before us, someone who is often much different (and usually much more complex and interesting) than our image of her."[165]

Indeed, each of our daughters is unique, complex, and interesting. By communicating always our confidence in girls, by stepping back so they can develop their intellectual maturity and resilience, and by not insisting that they live our dreams, we allow them to be prepared and free to live their own.

Tips & Tactics

Allow your daughter to learn from failure. When you let her experience the consequences of her decision making, you are teaching her to be independent. As long as you are willing to rescue your daughter, she has no reason to learn how to think in advance about the outcomes of the choices she makes.

• • •

Sometimes we can overpower our daughters with *our* dreams for their lives. Some girls will resist the takeover, but others acquiesce to avoid upset or to please. Our job is to steer clear of transplanting our goals into our daughters' visions, lest we lengthen the time required for them to learn to take charge of their lives.

40. Gunsmoke in the Garage
Gender-Neutral Nurturing

Reading an article recently about new research that suggested that we nurture girls and boys differently, I remembered seeing the photograph of Dad sitting in a chair, looking very proud, holding a football on which someone had written, "It's a boy!" This was obviously right after my brother, Tom, was born. I wonder what Dad was holding when they took a photograph of him after I was born, I thought. So I called my mom and asked her. "Well, you see, it was entirely different. Your dad was just getting out of the army when you were born. There was no time for him to be thinking about things like that," she responded. "Well, what do you think he would have been holding had there been time?" I asked. "Hmmm, I don't have any idea," she said.

As I tried to gain perspective and resist rushing to the conclusion that having a boy called for more celebration than having a girl, I remembered that in those early years, when Tom was still a baby, I did things with Dad that other fathers would usually do with a son. In other words, Dad was fairly gender neutral in how he interacted with me. He called me his Saturday helper, and every Saturday morning we had a list of tasks—repairs, building projects, errands to run. I can recall long stretches spent in the garage, Dad at the workbench while I was doing whatever it was a seven-year-old could do, and both of us listening to *Gunsmoke* on the radio. Years later, when I was out on my own, Dad bought me a toolbox "for those small repairs you'll be doing," and when I was well into adulthood, he coached me through laying a plywood floor in the attic.

It would appear that Dad did me a favor by including me in what would typically be male activities. How we interact and socialize children from the time they are born has long-term implications for behaviors, says neurologist Lise Eliot in her book *Pink Brain, Blue Brain: How Small Differences Grow into Troublesome Gaps—and What We Can Do about It.* According to a *Newsweek* review of the book, several "disguised-gender experiments have shown that adults perceive baby boys and girls differently, seeing identical behavior through a gender-tinted lens."[166] One such study revealed that mothers of baby girls underestimated by nine degrees the angle of the incline their eleven-month-old daughters could crawl down, whereas mothers of boys were accurate to within one degree. The conclusion Eliot draws is that when we project those limitations onto a girl, we set in motion a self-fulfilling prophecy. We create different experiences for her than we create for a boy, and those experiences leave "footprints on the very structure and function of the brain," thus leading to gender differences in adult behavior.[167]

Although I do not believe that nurture is the only cause of the divergence in behaviors we see between adolescent girls and boys, I am clear that when we signal to girls that we underestimate their ability to manage their lives, we encourage them to do the same. It is very easy for a girl to take to heart our reluctance to confirm her maturity and competency. When she senses our doubt, she integrates it into her opinion of herself, steps back from taking the kinds of healthy risks that lead to success, and is blind to the strength and proficiency within her.

Self-doubt will follow a young woman into college and her career. The results of a recent study of female and male managers from a range of industries across the country revealed that men "slightly overestimated how their bosses would rate them," while the women managers studied "underestimated their ratings on average by 11 percent."[168] The implications of these findings are far-reaching and contribute, as the authors of the study noted, to women "creating their own glass ceilings."[169]

Girls are far less likely to have a collision with a ceiling of self-doubt when they develop a bedrock belief in their own competence as they prepare for the rigors of higher education. As parents and educators, we need to challenge girls to reach further. We need to leave no doubt that we know they will reach their goals, if not at first, then later with more effort. We give them permission to make mistakes so they will have practice in recovering. Finally, we coach girls in how to initiate the changes they want to make in their lives by insisting that they become experts in seeking the constructive criticism that allows them to develop clarity about where they shine and where more skill building is required.

Tips & Tactics

Be aware of ways that you may be unintentionally underestimating your daughter's maturity or readiness to undertake a task. If you are raising a son and a daughter, take note of how you may communicate differently with each child. How do you respond when your daughter encounters a setback? Do you respond the same way to a son in a similar situation? What are your expectations for your daughter when there is a problem she needs to solve? Do you have different expectations for your son?

41. The Tallest Oak
Providing an Environment for Success

When I was growing up, no one could have anticipated the impact of parents who provided family get-togethers, frequent conversation, engagement in children's interests, and occasional wise interventions on their behalf. Indeed, my family would have been astonished to discover that parenting behavior like theirs has been studied and formulated. My great-aunt Nettie showered me with attention; my dad read the Sunday funnies to me every week; dinner conversation with my brother and parents every night centered on our teachers and on what we had learned that day; my parents supported my piano lessons and incessant piano practicing through the years; my mom intervened when my old-style piano teacher created an atmosphere that was too intense for me at my age.

All of these were spontaneous gestures that reflected the values of family life in a small midwestern town. But according to Malcolm Gladwell in his book *Outliers: The Story of Success*, it amounted to "concerted cultivation," a parenting style identified by sociologist Annette Lareau as an attempt to actively "foster and assess a child's talent, opinions, and skills."[170] This approach, Gladwell says, has "enormous advantages" because children learn "teamwork . . . [and] how to cope in highly structured settings [and] interact comfortably with adults."[171] These children have a "social savvy," what psychologist Robert Sternberg calls *practical intelligence*, that is, "knowing what to say to whom, knowing when to say it, and knowing how to say it for maximum effect."[172] My mother had her own label for that skill set—knowing "how to do."

Gladwell's thesis in *Outliers* is that there are complex reasons why some people are successful and why others, with equally innate gifts, are not. What is particularly true, he says, is that there is not a direct correlation between intellectual IQ and success.[173] One has to be "smart enough," but after that point is reached, there is more to the story.[174] Two people who are equally intelligent may vary greatly in the level of success attained. In order to understand why this is true, we must look at the environments in which individuals develop. It is "the values of the world we inhabit and the people we surround ourselves with," Gladwell writes, who have "a profound effect on who we are."[175]

Columnist David Brooks recently commented on Gladwell's theory and opined that individual will, resilience, perseverance, and the ability to focus one's attention *are* powerful determinants in one's destiny.[176] I tend to agree with that, especially since I am the daughter of midwesterners who did create much success through individual hard work, resolve, and innate intelligence. That being said, those of us who teach wholeheartedly endorse Gladwell's notion that surrounding adolescents with rich opportunities and sustained engagement with adults who inspire and encourage them changes the lives of these teens and sets them on a path to success and purpose.

When mothers engage with their daughters' interests and are, themselves, strong role models or when dads are aspirational for their daughters and support their ambitions, parents are tailoring environments conducive to girls' healthy growth. They are essentially teaching a girl how to "customize" her environment for her "best purposes."[177]

One of Gladwell's analogies sharpens our understanding of the power of an environment conducive to optimum growth. The tallest oak in the forest, he says, outpaces the surrounding trees "not just because it grew from the hardiest acorn . . . [but] also because no other trees blocked its sunlight, the soil . . . was . . . rich, no rabbit chewed through its bark . . . , and no lumberjack cut it down."[178]

Miss Hall's School is one example of a sun-filled, hardy spot where girls thrive. By engaging with girls, coaching them in how to advocate for themselves, seeking their opinions, and providing opportunities that they can leverage for their own purposes and for the work they do together, we create a community that, to use Gladwell's expression, "prepares them properly for the world."[179] A recent alumna described in an e-mail the gift this community gave her. "When I first arrived at MHS, I never thought that I would graduate the person I am today. I want to lead. I want to follow. I want to help people. Most of all, I want to go out into the world and learn everything I can . . . so that one day I will be able to speak and inspire others the way you have inspired me."[180] This young woman is poised perfectly for success.

Tips & Tactics

It is not enough that parents provide a home environment that inspires their daughter to engage with others around shared values and interests. Her peer group must do the same. If the priorities of your daughter's friends diverge significantly from those you aspire to for her, look around for ways to redirect her. Joining her in volunteer work is one of the best ways to foster her self-worth and to expand the number of strong role models in her life.

42. Self-Adjustment in Operation
Support in a Time of Change

Things didn't always suit me when I was growing up in Joplin, Missouri. I can remember, for example, the car breaking down one summer, less than twenty-four hours into our vacation. Waiting on the side of the road for the tow truck to rescue us, I grumbled about how boring it was going to be sitting around in a hot Minnesota car-repair garage. Then there were the sneakers. I really needed the ones at Ramsey's, the cool ones like all my friends had. Mom had other plans. "The ones at Penney's are just as good," she announced. Never mind that the rubber around the edge was way too wide. Never mind that I'd be the laughingstock of my class.

I can see myself, scowl on my face, not interested in trying very hard to accept setbacks and disappointments as a young teen. Fortunately, as it turned out for me, Mom and Dad weren't too interested in accepting crankiness. When I got crabby, Mom would always say, "You need to sweeten up." Dad's advice was, "Straighten up and fly right." What they were really suggesting was that I needed to self-adjust.

A few months ago, I stood in front of the copier in the library here at Miss Hall's School. Being the first to use the machine that morning, I had just turned it on and was watching the screen as it began to operate: Please Wait. Copier Is Warming Up. There were a few whirring noises, and the screen announced, Please Wait. Self-Adjustment in Operation. Then a few thumps, and finally, Ready to Copy. My first thought was that anything that self-adjusts, without any help from me, is a friend of mine. My second thought, however, was that adolescent girls frequently need to self-adjust, and our job as teachers and parents is to stand by and wait.

Every girl who arrives at her school on opening day, whether she is a new girl or a returning student, is heading into a period of adjustment. Ninth graders will begin a new chapter in their lives and will face the academic challenges of high school for the first time. All new girls, regardless of grade level, will adjust to a new school culture, new friends, and new teachers. But even returning students will adjust to a new grade and the loss of summer's leisure schedule.

In addition to adjusting to changes in the outer world, girls between the ages of thirteen and eighteen must also adjust constantly to changes within. A girl entering the middle adolescent years (ages thirteen to fifteen) must say good-bye to the middle-school self she knew so well. She forms a very clear idea of herself in middle school. As she makes the transition to a high-school curriculum, develops physically, deals with emerging sexual energy, shifts into a higher cognitive area with more abstract thinking required, interacts with older students, and loses old friends and makes new ones, she can feel quite fragile about who she really is. She may miss the younger middle-school girl she used to be and experience a period of difficult self-adjustment as she struggles to find a vision for the high-school self.

However, regardless of where girls are in their journey toward adulthood, they are continuously being asked to self-adjust and realign their changing selves with a changing world. Consider how many new ideas are being introduced into their lives and how susceptible they are to being taken by surprise. They simply haven't lived long enough and the cognitive functions haven't expanded far enough to allow them to anticipate possible outcomes. Change and newness await them at every turn. Their only option is to make the necessary alterations, but it is not easy work, and it is often accompanied by a good bit of teenage angst.

What can we as adults do to support girls during this stage? First, we have to remind ourselves what the shifting sands of adolescence feel like. The next time your daughter is out of sorts, imagine this: You cruise out of your driveway one morning, and everyone is driving on the left side of the road. At the corner, the stoplights are gone, and there are digital commands you don't understand. When you stop to ask someone what has happened, the person speaks a language you've never heard. It seems that all the rules have changed, and no one invited you to the meeting. That is how our daughters feel much of the time.

Second, the most important support we can offer is our belief that an adolescent girl can and will self-adjust, just like the copier. Furthermore, she needs us to stand by. We will provide emotional support and guide her gently by asking her how she plans to approach a situation. But our job is not to grab the toolbox and start to fix things ourselves. We should be prepared for some whirring of emotions and angry thumps as she makes her necessary modifications, but these are not causes for concern. Over time, as we know, she will learn to adjust to life's challenges with the grace and confidence that only come from years of practice.

Adolescence is a time for adjustment. Have patience, and stand by.

Tips & Tactics

The next time your daughter is going through an unsteady time, perhaps reacting to a setback or dealing with other changes, resist the urge to overidentify with her upset. Privately, recall similar times when you were her age, but avoid acting on your feelings about those times. By doing that, you are giving her the space she needs to self-adjust.

43. Dale Evans Revisited
Spotlighting Strong Role Models

When I was eight, play didn't begin until my friends and I had made some basic decisions. "Who will you be?" we'd ask each other. Nurse? Patient? Teacher? Mother? Cowgirl? Once we knew the general outline of the pretend world we were about to create, we could fill in the props, be they neighborhood children or the plastic stethoscope and syringe in the bright red nurse's kit. My personal favorite was cowgirl. I kept my (pretend) gun and holster in the bottom drawer of the desk in my room. When my brother would yell, "There's been a robbery at the bank!" I'd grab my gun and cowgirl hat and jump on the horse (broom) I kept handy in the corner. Being a mother was the fallback choice in the many games of pretend; I could do that with just my dolls, even without friends to join in.

As I think back on what I could imagine was possible as I envisioned my future over fifty years ago, I can see that the options—mom, teacher, nurse, cowgirl (thanks to Dale Evans)—were few, but they had more substance than what much of our culture holds out for girls today. The culture is filled with inane, goofy examples of what it means to be a woman, and there is no shortage of passive princess role models parading across the consumer stage for our young girls. Barbie continues to have an iron grip on the top spot for most popular toy for girls, and a quick visit to Barbie's website is all it takes to know that tiaras, mermaid tails, and stilettos are the most frequently used images to teach girls what it means to be female.[181] While boys are invited to check out cameras, fast-moving cars, and action figures on one toymaker's website, girls are invited to enter "precious places" and "meet the princesses."[182]

It's tempting to think that the fantasy world a child creates is an inconsequential part of growing up. Pretend play, however, is about role-playing on the way to formulating future life choices. As we all know, when a child assumes the identity of a pretend character, she *is* that person. In the mindset of her new role, she creates language and dialogue, acts out thoughts, and solves problems. Borders between the real and pretend worlds vanish. Patterns established with such depth and determination are not inconsequential. In my own case, I may have been on a broom, but I *was* the heroic Dale Evans bolting out the side door of my house in search of the bad guys.

Girls of all ages need competent, smart role models to dream about and pretend to be. Our job as parents and teachers is to resist offering girls the ornamental and helpless female images that stream forth from too much of our pop culture. It is brave and compassionate women that our daughters need to see, and it is our job as teachers and parents to make certain that they see them. At Miss Hall's School, we continually present images of strong women through academic subjects; through presentations, assemblies, and special events; and through real-life role models. As parents, we need to talk to our daughters about the women in our families, about their lives, about the challenges they faced through a world war or through raising a family in difficult times. We need to pass along the family stories of courage that are our family legacies.

An example of how girls respond to a cultural image that presents great possibilities for their lives occurred a few years ago at the school. Several of us, girls and adults, had gathered to watch the premiere of *Commander in Chief*, a television drama series about the first woman to occupy the Oval Office. The day after the episode aired, one girl, wide-eyed with enthusiasm, stopped me in the hall. "Wow!" she exclaimed. "When they announced 'the President of the United States' and Geena

Davis walked through the door, I had tears in my eyes."

Former US Surgeon General Joycelyn Elders has said, "You can't be what you don't see."[183] We might expand this thought to say that too often our daughters are limited by what they *do* see. Our responsibility as adults is to make certain that girls have had glimpses of women doing great and important work. Such exposure during the teen years gives girls something new to picture as they form the thoughts that will transform their lives.

Tips & Tactics

Girls need to emulate strong role models, not the weak, self-indulgent personalities that are so abundant in popular culture. Talk to your daughter about the lives of the women and men in your family and how they managed life's difficulties. Those stories of courage are your daughter's legacy.

•••

Ask your daughter whom she would honor if she were to give her own Distinguished Person Award. Suggest that she choose someone she knows, rather than a celebrity or historical figure. What are the qualities she would reference in her award presentation? What examples would she give of how the award recipient has demonstrated those qualities?

44. Have Some Potatoes
Shared Community Purpose

During supper, when Dad would say, "Have some potatoes," he was really asking me to pass the bowl his way. My brother and I knew the routine, and we also knew that it was impolite to have a second helping before passing the bowl to Dad. My friends, however, didn't know the drill. They would respond with a "No, thank you" to Dad's rhetorical comment and have to be told to send the requested item in his direction. And if they reached for another potato as the bowl went by, Dad didn't hesitate to point out their faux pas.

I spent a good bit of time explaining to my friends that Dad really liked them, even though he didn't think twice about offering parental advice any time they were at my house. He wasn't alone. When I visited at my friends' homes or those of other adults who knew my family, I was just as likely to be corrected as when I was with my own parents.

In spite of the popular sentiment that it takes a village to raise a child, the vast majority of parents today want nothing to do with giving tune-up talks to the offspring of others. In a *Wall Street Journal* article, author Jeffrey Zaslow reports on a Michigan teen whose parents require her car to sport a bumper sticker asking, How's My Teen Driving?[184] The bumper sticker includes a number to call to report reckless behavior. The father who dreamed up the campaign admits that it's been difficult to build a subscription because parents are skittish about getting involved with other people's children.

Zaslow suggests three reasons for our hesitancy.[185] First, parents are defensive. We live in a culture where perfection has great currency. We're highly invested in parenting perfectly and having children who don't misbehave. Who's going to risk scolding someone else's child at a time when, as Zaslow says, parents think that "any criticism reflects poorly on them"?[186] Second, parents are overprotective. Our impulse to interact with a youngster can be quickly overruled when we remember that we could be easily perceived as a potential predator. Finally, Zaslow notes that parents are indulgent and are not at all interested in allowing other adults to tamper with their child's self-esteem by correcting poor behavior.

However, there is another reason we keep our distance: we are living in a time when social constructs are brittle and wobbly. The feeling of shared community purpose and values that defined the experience of my parents in the fifties and that encouraged all adults to parent all children is rarely found today. We live side-by-side with strangers whose value systems may not match our own. We can't partner with extended families because they often live miles, even continents, away. We're so spent when we finish our long work days that there is no energy left to socialize as we used to in church or neighborhood gatherings. In other words, the number of people with whom we are in relationship is minimal; as a result, the level of trust in and responsibility to others that defined our parents' lives is also minimal.

When trust unravels from our social fabric, fear takes its place, and it is our children who lose out most. In *The Shelter of Each Other: Rebuilding Our Families to Enrich Our Lives*, Mary Pipher writes that aspects of the American culture, such as the invasion of technology, isolation through demographic changes, the negative influence of the media and corporations, and crime in neighborhoods result in a climate where "parents worry about their children's physical safety and children are afraid of strangers."[187] In a way, we've all been hijacked, pulled away from one of the central roles of families throughout history, which is, as Pipher describes it, to "help . . . children connect with a meaningful world outside the family."[188] It becomes harder and harder for our daughters to form those connections when we are suspicious and wary of what's lurking beyond the front door.

However, girls need connection because it is the conduit to their learning. Girls thrive in environments where webs of relationships provide reliable structures. They flourish where there is an array of adults they can trust and who are willing to be involved in their lives. In a connected community, girls are free to be themselves and excel.

In connected settings, girls also learn that they can depend on the adults around them to respond honestly to their actions. Just as I benefited from the pointers I received from adults in my parents' social sphere, girls today benefit when they are surrounded by consistent messages about how to manage in the world. It is also true that girls often hear messages more clearly when delivered by nonparent adults because those messages are freer of the emotionally charged signals that can create barriers in parent-child communication. What is essential is that we provide girls with a web of connections, for it is in that environment that girls deepen their understanding of what makes trust possible and learn that the strength of community lies in the delicate balance between freedom and responsibility.

Tips & Tactics

A strong peer group is important, but it is not a substitute for an adult-rich environment (school, religious community, or extended family). If connections with strong adult role models are missing or in short supply in your daughter's life, import those connections. Volunteer with your daughter at an assisted living center or "adopt" grandparents with whom you both can visit. These connections will nurture her sense of self-worth and enrich her life.

45. Remember When?
Reflecting on Childhood Memories

Holiday gatherings have a way of encouraging families to reminisce. You may have noticed that conversations around the holiday dinner table include a lot of "Remember when we . . ." If your children are anything like mine, they often recall events that you have absolutely no memory of. And have you noticed how animated they are when they recount every last detail? How can events that seem to have made lasting impressions and perhaps even were formative experiences not have registered with us?

I have listened with stunned disbelief as my daughters have portrayed me to friends as a kind of health-food zealot who raised them entirely on twigs and leaves. "Exaggeration!" I say. I do remember sending granola bars and apples instead of cupcakes to school when one daughter turned seven, but I know my children were no strangers to Wendy's. I like to think of myself as a flexible health-food zealot.

My children also remember summer afternoons when we unfolded a quilt under the apple tree in the backyard and they each picked out three books for us to read together. Some of the good times they recall I have no memory of whatsoever. I always take credit nonetheless.

I have to admit that it worried me that I had forgotten so much. However, an article by Sue Shellenbarger in the *Wall Street Journal* confirmed that this phenomenon of not recognizing your children's memories seems to happen to many parents.[189] She writes that when English teacher Christina Looper Baker and her daughter, Christina Baker Kline, wrote *The Conversation Begins: Mothers and Daughters Talk about Living Feminism*, a collection of essays by prominent mothers and daughters on their lives together, several mother-daughter pairs dropped out because they couldn't agree on their memories.[190]

Shellenbarger decided to do some research on this topic. She discovered that there are some common themes in what adult children recall from their childhoods. Memories that have to do with cementing a one-on-one bond, for example, are frequently mentioned.[191]

I decided to test her theory, so I called my younger daughter. Without giving too much away, I asked her what memories came to mind from when she was a little girl. Sure enough, right on cue, she said, "I remember driving to school with you every day. I got to sit in the front seat. We turned on the radio and sang together. You listened to what I had to say. I felt like an adult." Of course, I remember driving us to school, but I had no idea it meant so much to her. I have to admit that when she described how she felt, all I could think was, phew! I did something right!

Another common thread in childhood memories is how often the big events get passed over. My daughter volunteered that when she and her friends reminisce about growing up, "It's never about the big vacation. It's the simple, everyday stuff."

I decided to call my older daughter, who was less intrigued by my research project. But she humored me for five minutes. She recalled "Grandma sitting with me until I fell asleep," adding that her father and I weren't always interested in that routine. I started to say that I didn't remember that she wanted anyone to sit with her, but I changed my mind. The point seemed to be security, another theme Shellenbarger identified. And under the no-experience-is-too-small category, my daughter remembered sitting under a dogwood tree in the front yard, "feeling like I was in my own cave with moss for my carpet." I have heard her talk about that dogwood tree before with almost a hushed reverence for the calmness it afforded her. As I think back on those days, I remember watching her from the window and noting that she was safe. But I had no idea of the magic she was creating in that special place.

Shellenbarger quotes James A. Levine, one of the authors of *Working Fathers: New Strategies for Balancing Work and Family*. "For our kids, the extraordinary is in the ordinary," he says.[192] Shellenbarger adds, "Noticing the magic in kids' ordinary moments requires a mindfulness often rare in modern life."[193]

Reflecting on our own childhood from time to time is a good exercise, regardless of our age. What is our first memory? Is it about feeling secure or creating a bond with someone? My very earliest memory is about being at a picnic with my parents. A violent storm came up, and we all had to run inside for cover. I remember how safe I felt sitting next to my mother. Again, security is the theme.

It is easy to become so busy being adults that we fall out of touch with our kids. Life is hectic, but maybe our resolution should be to take more time to recall the vivid memories of our past. By so doing, we nurture the mindfulness it takes to be a truly thoughtful parent.

Tips & Tactics

What are your most vivid memories from childhood, and what are the basic feelings associated with those memories? Security? Validation? Connection? The next time you feel overwhelmed with your daughter's needs, wants, and ups and downs, refocus on what she will remember: connections with you that confirm her self-worth and encourage her independence.

PART THREE:

Navigating Unhealthy Landscapes

46. Powerful Ideas
Shifting the Focus from Societal Expectations

We weren't pressured to look sexy at Joplin Senior High School back in the sixties. Pretty was important, nice was a must, but provocative was never. We worked at *not* revealing more than what was considered appropriate. We wore collared blouses tucked into our skirts. There was protection in layers. Slips went under blouses; sweaters went over. Skirts were a modest inch above the knee. Hosiery was required. The only risks we took were those that might involve snagging a run in our stockings before the last class of the day was over.

Society at that time was more than satisfied with our being "good" girls, and we simply weren't subjected to the sexually charged air that pulses just below the radar in high schools today. If anything in the curriculum was remotely sexual when I was in high school, we stared at the floor. The day we read from Walt Whitman's "Song of Myself" in English class, "Tenderly will I use you, curling grass; / It may be you transpire from the breasts of young men," heat poured from my red face.[194] We went about our lives insulated, comparatively speaking, from the temptations of the adult world.

Today's girls are pressured to look and act older than they are, to adopt a provocative persona modeled relentlessly in our culture. When that pressure is combined with the demands to be thin, beautiful, and successful in school, a girl finds herself in a very high-stakes game for approval. In fact, the stakes are so high that greater numbers of girls than ever before are finding unhealthy ways to escape. *USA Today* presented findings from the 2009 Partnership Attitude Tracking Study indicating that "two-thirds of teen girls reported that using drugs helps kids cope with problems at home, and half said drugs help teens forget troubles."[195] The study also showed that unlike alcohol use by boys, alcohol use by girls has undergone a significant increase and that marijuana use by girls has increased at almost twice the rate as marijuana use by boys.[196] Furthermore, the findings remind us that the reasons for teen substance abuse differ along gender lines. Boys experiment for the thrill of it and to have fun and relax; girls abuse drugs and alcohol for reasons related to stress and low self-esteem.[197]

Adding to the alarm over this new trend is the tendency for alcohol abuse to go hand-in-hand with sexual activity.[198] Studies have shown the correlation between sexual intimacy at a young age and depression later in life.[199] In other words, adopting adult behaviors as a way to escape the pressures in their lives increases teens' risks of having emotional difficulties as adults.

Society's obsession with sexuality and external flawlessness swirls around girls. Over time, it is difficult for them to resist believing that these qualities are their primary source of power. Most importantly, they *will* believe it unless an equally potent new idea is presented, that is, unless an intervention occurs.

The locus of control for girls' lives cannot reside in the mass media. For girls to reclaim their authentic selves and to reconnect to their dreams, they must learn that the best high one can have is from being in charge of one's life. When we teach a girl how to advocate for herself, to speak out about what matters to her, to solve problems, and to make choices aligned with her values and long-term goals, we are helping her build a source for her power that is authentic and reliable and that will lead to a lifetime of emotional well being. When authenticity is the source of a girl's power, she is free.

Tips & Tactics

Take stock of where in your daughter's life she is able to advocate for what she truly believes. What causes does she support? How involved in those causes is she? Are there problems in her community that she would like to see fixed? Does she have ideas for how she might solve the problems? Can she take action on those ideas? In order to resist the shallow messages coming to girls through the popular culture, girls must experience new ways to be powerful.

47. Leading with the Mind
Sexuality and Cultural Messages

We didn't talk much about sex when I was growing up. At school, we studied the reproductive organs in single-gender health classes. At home, my mother made sure I understood the physical changes that occurred as I made my way through puberty. But detailed discussions about the new "equipment" that my teenage friends and I were developing and how we might use it didn't happen. Of course, adults also weren't talking openly about sex. Love and marriage, yes. But not sex. Remember *I Love Lucy*? Bedroom scenes featured twin beds, and the stars were required to have at least one foot on the floor at all times.

Times have changed. Our culture is saturated with sex. Recently, I stood in front of a display of teen magazines and noted how often the word *sex* appeared. Sizzling headlines on glossy covers asked "Are You Sexy?" or proclaimed "Sexy Minis," "Sexy Scene Stealers," and "Sexy Hair." More headlines focused girls on everything but their brains: "Jeans That Give the Best Butt," "Be a Great Kisser," "365 Ways to Look Hot," and "Get Flatter Abs in Two Weeks." Television also leaves little to the imagination. According to industry statistics, the number of sexual scenes on television, across all genres, "has nearly doubled since 1998," and a staggering "70 percent of all shows include some sexual content, and . . .

these shows average 5.0 sexual scenes per hour."[200] Moving to the Internet creates a more disturbing picture. Analysis of entertainment found online, for example in video games, makes it clear that females are frequently portrayed as sex objects or as the targets of sexual violence.[201]

To add to the problem, we're exposing children to provocative images at increasingly younger ages. Amidst controversy, Mattel discontinued Lingerie Barbie and her "heavenly bustier ensemble," but the popular Bratz dolls with their flirty, seductive looks and sexy clothing (miniskirts and fishnet stockings) keep sexualized images in front of girls as young as four. The report of the American Psychological Association's Task Force on the Sexualization of Girls specifically noted, regarding Bratz dolls, that it is "worrisome when dolls designed specifically for 4- to 8-year-olds are associated with an objectified adult sexuality."[202]

What is particularly alarming about our culture's sexualization of children is its occurrence at a time when we are seeing the onset of puberty at younger ages than ever before. One in six eight-year-old girls is entering puberty, compared with one in one hundred a century ago. Researchers seeking causes are looking at possible connections to, among others, the increase of obesity in children, hormones in food, and phthalates, "a ubiquitous chemical plasticiser" found in products as diverse as building materials, food packaging, garden hoses, and shoe soles.[203] The problem, says Lynn Ponton in *The Romance of Risk: Why Teenagers Do the Things They Do*, is that girls can have "fully developed women's bodies with all the associated social commentary before they even enter adolescence."[204] In other words, girls' physical development launches them into sexual orbit long before they're emotionally mature enough to manage the social pressures that result.

As if this were not troublesome enough, society compounds the situation by sending girls distorted messages about how their emerging sexuality is related to their self-worth and personal power. According to the report of the American Psychological Association's Task Force on the Sexualization of Girls, "Research suggests that viewing material that is sexually objectifying can contribute to body dissatisfaction, eating disorders, low self-esteem, depressive affect, and even physical health problems in high-school-aged girls and in young women."[205]

Of course, the source of a young woman's healthy sense of self is not a low-cut blouse or a short skirt. Girls will benefit when adults can take steps to slow down the pace at which adolescents are being hurled into provocative adult behaviors. Furthermore, our daughters' genuine confidence and self-esteem will develop as a result of our spending time to help them make sense of a culture that pushes every sexual boundary and depicts sex "as recreation, sex as commerce and exploitation, sex as sport, status, and even violence."[206] The code of silence in effect when I was a teen won't work today. We must talk to girls early and often about what they are experiencing as they develop. If we can't find the words, there are resources to help us. Author and human sexuality educator Deborah Roffman reminds us what research in sex education consistently confirms: "Children who grow up in families where sexuality is openly discussed grow up healthier."[207]

Tips & Tactics

It has always been a parent's responsibility to help a teen understand the fallacies in the messages communicated through popular culture. Ask your daughter to make a list of her personal qualities and of the evidence that she does indeed possess them. By redirecting her to reflect upon the inner strengths and talents that will shape the course of her life, you dilute the impact of the diminishing messages that surround her.

48. The Objective Case
Countering Media Imagery

My magazine of choice in both my junior and senior high-school years was *Seventeen*, and I would disappear for a couple of hours when a new edition showed up in our mailbox. There were essential tips on dating, friendships, makeup, and hair, but I particularly loved the fashion sections—Peter Pan-collared shirts, scoop-neck blouses, dyed-to-match outfits, net petticoats, hip-pleated skirts, and circular skirts with appliqués. This magazine and others in our house (*Life, Saturday Evening Post, Ladies' Home Journal*) were full of stuff to buy and people selling it, but the girls and women pictured were whole, with all body parts intact.

Things have changed. I walked through Miss Hall's School's library recently and noticed the display our librarian had created under the heading, "See the Pretty Book Covers." Below that was the question, "Notice anything interesting?" and the answer, "All the women are headless or their heads are cut in half." The display included several dozen books with covers of females with no head visible or with only part of a head in the picture. There are several ways one might explain this vogue in cover designs, but the trend in advertising to feature pieces of a woman, instead of the whole person, is clear. Scan today's teen and popular-culture magazines and note the number of times that women and girls appear not only without faces but also as only body parts (mostly breasts, buttocks, and legs). The subliminal and powerful message to our daughters is you are a thing, not a person.

The objectification of women is an epidemic in our society, and it is almost inevitable that our girls and young women will connect in some way with the warped images. In their book *So Sexy, So Soon: The New Sexualized Childhood and What Parents Can Do to Protect Their Kids,* authors Diane E. Levin and Jean Kilbourne discuss the onslaught of messages in our culture that objectify and sexualize our children. Images that would have been labeled as pornography when I was a teen are everywhere girls look: on billboards, in music videos and teen publications, and on the Internet. Because these images are so prevalent, girls are at risk for absorbing the visual toxins without giving them a second thought. "Once something becomes normalized," says Cordelia Anderson, an expert in the prevention of the sexual exploitation of children, "it becomes the wallpaper of our existence—we don't see it, we accept it as just the way it is and we are numbed to seeing any ill effects or taking action to change it."[208]

It is our job as parents and teachers to make certain that girls are *not* numb to the images that diminish them. Levin and Kilbourne refer to research that indicates that girls' exposure to sexualized images in the mass media "made girls think of and treat their own bodies as sexual objects."[209] This self-objectification, they add, "has a host of negative emotional consequences. . . . [It can] lead to feelings of disgust about one's body."[210] It is essential that we talk with girls about the images they encounter and help them see that their value as individuals has nothing to do with their size or shape. In addition, we want girls to understand that so many of the advertising campaigns targeted at them are all about selling them products to make girls into *perfect objects.*

It is also our job to support girls in discovering another subtle but powerfully limiting message in advertising, which is that females are objects to be *acted upon.* Cultural anthropologist Scott A. Lukas, who created the Gender Ads Project, notes that males in advertising are often represented as decision makers, whereas females are passive.[211] (It is difficult to imagine anything more passive than being headless.) So much of what girls face in cultural imagery every day is about not being in charge of or having agency in their own lives.

Girls are eager to examine these media messages. At Miss Hall's School, a group of girls has been investigating how women are portrayed in the mass media. They demonstrated the many ways women are represented and then posed questions for other girls to ponder. What are the messages in a particular advertisement? What role does the woman play in that ad? Is there a difference in how women and men are shown in that video? Why is it that images for male Olympic athletes communicate proficiency, power, and achievement, while those for female Olympians often include passive, coquettish, or provocative depictions?

We cannot stand by while the marketing industry sells our girls a bill of dismembered goods. Our responsibility is to intervene and inspire teens to envision themselves as whole young women, ready to lead with their intellects, creativity, and compassion. Supported by parents and teachers who are enlightened and savvy, girls will cultivate robust and full images of the purposeful lives they will lead.

Tips & Tactics

Suggest that your daughter and her friends collect some information about how women and girls are portrayed in the mass media. Checking out the covers of teen magazines at the grocery store, noting how women are represented in magazines about sports, and surveying the book covers at a local bookstore should prompt your daughter to ask why those images have been chosen. What are the advertisers saying about women and girls through their choices of dress, camera angle, poses, and facial expressions? Are boys and men portrayed the same way as girls and women? Your daughter may become so interested in the topic that she will decide to create a video or start a blog about what she has discovered.

49. Resisting Media Messages
Pushing Back against Depictions of Sex and Violence

The Saturday night lineup included *Perry Mason*, *Your Hit Parade*, and *Gunsmoke*, and it was the best family time of the week when I was growing up. Mom would make hamburgers and potato salad. We would fix our plates and head to the big bedroom, my parents' room, where the only TV in the house was located. Even when I was old enough to date, I would often feign a babysitting job when a beau called just so I wouldn't miss Saturday night at home.

Perry Mason, Della Street, Kitty, Doc, Marshal Dillon—they were a tame bunch, Main Street shoot-outs notwithstanding. My parents, my little brother, and I could all watch together, Mom and Dad not giving a thought about the possibility that our morals would be corrupted. And why would they have worried? In those days, good triumphed over evil, people were basically civil, and everyone was fully dressed.

Today, parents are worried about the impact of the mass media on young people, with good reason. I have heard parents voice their worry about how we can compete with the media blitz of negative messages directed toward girls, particularly those that promote provocative behaviors, meanness, materialism, and sexual violence against women. As we all know, any onetime "wardrobe malfunction" isn't any worse than what is available everywhere and all the time on television, on the Internet, in movies, and in magazines.

It has always been true that commercialism drives the media, and as marketers everywhere know, sex sells. Fifty years ago, however, we restrained ourselves to preserve postwar values of decency and our children's virtue. Perry and Della never wound up in bed together. With the sexual revolution of the seventies and the deregulation of the mass media industry in the eighties, though, we began hurtling down a slippery slope. Today, most taboos are gone, almost anything goes, and our daughters (and sons) are growing up in a violent and toxic environment that, as James P. Steyer writes in *The Other Parent: The Inside Story of the Media's Effect on Our Children,* "is not only destroying kids' innocence too soon but is also setting them up for disappointments and dangerous choices."[212]

As parents, we discuss with our daughters the unwanted consequences of being sexually active and the long-term value of postponing intimacy until one is emotionally ready. If these (and the wisdom of not dressing like the latest teen idol) were the only topics we needed to cover to counter the messages delivered by an out-of-control media culture, our job would be, if not easy, at least manageable. The fact is, however, that the stakes are much higher. A large portion of the messages delivered by the popular media are drenched in violence, and much of that violence is directed toward girls and women.

What do girls think about the images of violence that surround them? Over Sunday brunch here at Miss Hall's School, I posed this question to a group of girls. One girl said, "I know it gets into our subconscious." She's right. The research shows that repeated exposure creates a numbing effect and that we begin to accept physical aggression as "normal and tolerable."[213] Other girls responded by mentioning specific rap stars, whose graphic lyrics often express sexual and other physical violence toward women. The girls are not confused about what is driving this toxic phenomenon in our culture. "It's all about what sells," said one girl. And, if they had a daughter, would they allow her to watch or listen to these rappers? Without missing a beat, they responded in unison, "Absolutely not." Girls see the violence in our culture, but they believe, I suspect, that nothing can be done.

It is easy for all of us to feel powerless. After all, pushing back against a highly lucrative industry that knows very well that sex and violence sell products is not for the weak. However, the issue is too important to ignore. The world our children, both daughters and sons, experience today determines how they will envision their roles as leaders tomorrow. It is important that we take a hard look at violence in the media and that we do it through the lens of gender. "The issue is not just violence," write educators and activists Jackson Katz and Sut Jhally, "but the construction of violent masculinity as a cultural norm."[214]

Scan the popular culture that is all around you. As we all know, the mass media is saturated with ditzy, thinly clad, air-brushed females in provocative and often demeaning poses. But what are the messages associated with being male? "The male sports culture features regular displays of dominance and one-upmanship," write Katz and Jhally, and Hollywood sends the message loud and clear that "masculine power is embodied in muscle, firepower, and physical authority. . . . The culture produces a stream of images of violent, abusive men and promotes . . . dominance, power, and control as means of establishing . . . manhood."[215]

A sophisticated environment can push back against a popular culture that promulgates an unhealthy dynamic between women and men and shortchanges adolescents, both female and male. Girls need to be surrounded by adults who treat each other with respect, who are committed to sustaining a caring setting for all members of their community, and who illustrate that compassion, patience, and understanding are part of being a strong and competent adult.

It would be wonderful if we and our public media were working together to empower the next generation. We cannot fool ourselves, however, about the great divergence between the needs of adolescents and the perceived needs of advertisers. As teachers and parents, we can best fight back by continuing to develop awareness in ourselves and in our young people.

Tips & Tactics

Talk with your daughter about the violence she perceives in the mass media. You may not understand the words in her songs and videos, but she does. Ask her if she would allow a younger sister or friend to listen to the same music. Would she want her own daughter to see the images she sees? Most importantly, raise the promotion of violence as a topic that needs to be discussed and as a practice that cannot be seen as benign. Your courage to stand firm in how you view violence and cruelty in the media will be noticed by your daughter.

50. Aesop for Girls
Resolving Dissonant Assumptions

An old Doris Day movie ran on Turner Classic Movies not too long ago, and I was reminded of how infatuated I was with this star when I was young. I never missed her films when they played at the Fox or Paramount in my hometown. She was my hero, and my eight-by-ten black-and-white glossy photo of her was a prized possession. Of course, we were a little short on female heroes back in the fifties. There were Clara Barton and Madame Curie in textbooks, but somehow I never imagined myself being one of them. It was Doris Day for me. She had it all: beauty, pretty clothes, and handsome leading men. And now that I think about it, I was also attracted to a savvy quality and outspokenness that many of her characters exhibited. She always seemed to prevail in dinner-table discussions. Being beautiful as well as assertive and smart? Well, that was an intriguing idea, but one that raised conflicting notions in me as a girl.

Decades have passed since I tried as an adolescent to resolve this puzzle of how to value brains and appearance, but girls today have a similar challenge. Does smart plus pretty equal a date for Saturday night? Can I be popular and speak my mind? Can I be feminine and strong? Feminine and independent? Unfortunately, while there are many successful women and many excellent role models in our society, it is still the popular culture that provides the most visible, relentless, and problematic images.

Conflicting messages about womanhood abound. As parents and educators, we tell girls, "Be yourself. Own your dreams. You are amazing." These are powerful, big ideas that girls eagerly embrace. However, there is a cognitive dissonance that occurs for girls when they notice that females in the popular culture are too often associated with the weak, the frivolous, and the superficial. Given the amount of money expended annually in the United States to promote those images, we can assume that they enter a girl's consciousness with a mighty force and, at least for a time, are nearly irresistible.

The late columnist William Safire wrote about cognitive dissonance, the "nasty jangling" that occurs when one idea we have disagrees with another.[216] To resolve the dissonance, according to Safire, we make the weak cognition conform to the stronger one. As an example, he uses Aesop's fox. This fox saw a bunch of grapes and thought them delicious (Idea 1). He noticed, however, that they were too high on the vine for him to reach (Idea 2, and the stronger cognition). To resolve the clash of those two ideas, the fox determined that the grapes were sour and thus not worth the trouble. Safire uses this analogy to comment on issues in the political landscape, but it made me wonder how girls resolve the discord between our messages to them about being competent and authentic (Idea 1) and the media-driven representation of women as air-brushed fluff (Idea 2).

I gained insight when I discussed the topic with a few Miss Hall's School students. They agreed that there is a disconnect between the assumptions *they* are making about themselves and their futures and the assumptions about women put forth, for example, in reality TV. However, they also said that they reject the helpless and trivial representations of women when they encounter them and instead focus on being themselves. In other words, unlike the fox, these girls choose to resolve the dissonance by redoubling their efforts to reach the grapes. Girls have adopted ideas about their competence and authenticity as the stronger cognition.

These are capable girls who deliver an important message. They have been able to recognize the dominant cognition—that they have important work to do—and recognize it so completely that the subtleties of the distracting negative cognition—that they are just pretty faces—no longer pose a threat. As our girls find their way into young adulthood, they will no doubt continue to experience cognitive dissonance between who they believe they are and what some elements in the culture will tell them they should be. Their stronger cognition, however, is their confidence in their own strength, ability, and vision.

Tips & Tactics

Suggest that your daughter make a list of the most courageous (or the smartest) women alive today. Review her list with her, and ask her to explain why those women were chosen. Although we may think that girls have been taken in by the negative media that surrounds them, they may already be sorting through the conflicting messages. Your partnership in that endeavor will confirm for your daughter that she is on the right track.

51. Balancing the Scale
Body Image and Cultural Messages

Good Morning America is usually on in the background as I am getting ready for school. One morning, my ears perked up as I heard an editor for *Seventeen* magazine announce that the next month's issue would include clothes for plus sizes. With that lead-in, healthy-looking teenage girls walked on the set to model jeans, tops, and dresses that made them look good regardless of clothing size. But why the use of the word *plus*? It has that extra, over-the-top connotation. These girls had no extra pounds; they looked just right.

Glance at the females who are pictured in magazines from the late seventies. Catch a rerun of a TV show from the early eighties. You may be surprised at how our aesthetic sense of what is considered attractive in female bodies and shapes has changed. Go back to the fifties, and the difference is even more striking: Marilyn Monroe wore a size 16 dress. Today's female celebrities squeeze easily into a size 2 or 4.

Clinical psychologist Catherine Steiner-Adair has pointed out that the feminine ideal began to shift in the seventies with the prepubescent look of the model Twiggy.[217] Steiner-Adair says that the late seventies and the eighties added a business suit and weight lifting to the picture, and from the nineties we have a technologically manufactured woman, surgically altered and graphically airbrushed into an unnatural image.[218]

The impact of those unnatural images should be a concern for those who parent and teach girls. A YWCA report on the consequences of America's obsession with beauty notes that "women and girls cannot escape feeling judged on the basis of their appearance" when they are "engulfed by a popular culture saturated with images of idealized, air-brushed, and unattainable female physical beauty."[219] Advertising targeted at teenage girls as well as at women sends the message that if you don't like the body you were given, change it. And because the feminine ideal promulgated in the mass media is basically unattainable without considerable effort and expense, girls either feel that they fail to measure up or spend great amounts of energy and money dieting and shopping to fix what they see as a problem. It has been reported that the average American female is 5' 3.7" and weighs 152 pounds.[220] According to one Internet site advising young women how to enter the modeling business, the average female model is 5' 8" tall and weighs 108 to 125 pounds.[221]

By the time a girl is age thirteen or fourteen, she has been waging her battle with body-image issues for years. Studies show that 31 percent of nine-year-old girls fear being fat; 81 percent of ten-year-olds speak of feeling fat; and 50 percent of nine- and ten-year-olds say they feel better when they are on a diet.[222] "Preoccupation with thinness has become the norm rather than a pathology," says Steiner-Adair.[223]

What alarms those of us who teach girls is the knowledge, documented by studies such as Steiner-Adair's, that girls tend to measure their worth by what they see in the mirror and read on the scale. Our job is to put things back in balance by helping a girl to reconnect with the authentic power within her—the power that comes from her intellect, creativity, concern for others, and talent.

Adolescent girls need genuine role models that counter the invented, thinner-than-life versions on glossy pages. As parents and teachers, we can be such role models. We can ensure that girls are listened to and that their opinions are valued. Most importantly, we can recognize the need girls have to talk about the mixed cultural messages they receive and provide venues where girls can unpack the stereotypes in the media and engage in thoughtful discussions about their hopes and dreams. *Plus* has nothing to do with size and everything to do with the advantage of being in a place where girls come first.

Tips & Tactics

There is much focus on how the advertising industry distorts images of girls and women. The next time your daughter is assigned a research paper or essay, suggest that she investigate how women and girls or female athletes are portrayed in the mass media.

•••

Ask your daughter to list five things she would like to change about herself, and do the same for yourself. Look at the lists together. How many items reference a physical quality? Try making the list again with the rule that no physical features be mentioned.

52. Rites of Passage
Moving from Girlhood to Adulthood

When I saw the photograph of two skimpily dressed sweet-sixteen party girls in the *New York Times*, I gritted my teeth. The full-page report chronicled the craze in upscale, coming-of-age extravaganzas, some with price tags in five figures.[224] Pictured in the article were girls in outfits covering almost nothing. Their clothing, makeup, and hair gave them the seductive look of sultry twenty-five-year-olds.

I knew that some of the girls pictured were friends of Miss Hall's School students when they were all attending middle school together in Manhattan. I wondered what our students, now removed from New York's fast-paced social scene, thought of the article. It didn't seem to interest them much. Certainly their responses didn't begin to match my level of outrage. The few girls who spoke up wanted me to know that New York City isn't the only place where big parties take place.

What kind of party did you have when you turned sixteen? I think that was the year my parents let me have a boy-girl party in our living room, where all the lights were left on. Dressed in flats, dyed-to-match sweaters and skirts (ties and jackets for the guys), we played 45s, munched on chips, and drank pop.

I know that times have changed and that the mores of different regions vary, but does that mean common sense has to go out the window? Just because we're in a position to indulge our daughters, does that mean we should? Do adolescents really need parties that cost tens of thousands of dollars to celebrate living sixteen years? Why are we encouraging girls to mimic adult sophistication while still in their teens?

When I saw the *Times* photo, I thought of the title of David Elkind's book *The Hurried Child: Growing Up Too Fast Too Soon*. Those girls pictured in pink and black lace were clearly growing up too fast and too soon. I was also reminded of children's advocate Marian Wright Edelman and what she refers to as *affluenza*, by which she means the "empty materialism" that permeates our culture.[225] This is the condition we bestow on our daughters when we give them too much stuff.

Expanding on this theme of overindulgence, New York psychiatrist Pamela Sicher was quoted in the *Times* article as saying that privileged parents are "giving too much and requiring too little."[226] "There are too few challenges," she notes, "and children later have trouble figuring out what their worth is."[227]

The article's title, "A Sweet-16-Going-on-25 Party," suggests a rite of passage and made me think about growing up in modern society. Ours is not a culture in which ancient ceremonies officially escort our girls into adulthood. How does a girl today know when she is at last a full-fledged adult?

I decided to ask some Miss Hall's School students. Their responses were stories unique to each girl and her family. Several girls told me about quinceañera, a traditional coming-of-age ceremony celebrated when a Latina girl is fifteen. "The symbol is higher-heeled shoes," explained a student. She described how a family member, perhaps a godparent, hands the girl shoes on a pillow. "I felt different after that," she continued, "and my mother said, 'You're an adult now. I am stepping back. You must begin to make decisions on your own.'"

Other girls also used *stepping back* to describe the conscious attempt on the part of parents to give more freedom along with more responsibility. One student spoke about feeling that she had a larger role to play in "holding the household together." She felt important because she knew that others were depending on her. According to another girl, at a certain age her parents expected her to assume responsibility for all her finances. Several girls mentioned difficult situations or dilemmas they faced and how parents insisted that they work through them on their own. "My parents were still standing by," said one girl, "but I had to figure things out."

Wanting to learn more about formal rites of passage, I sought out a student who had experienced a bat mitzvah celebration. Because research has shown the positive impact of a bat mitzvah celebration on a girl's successful transition into adulthood, I was interested in this student's point of view.[228] "I was given more responsibility," she told me. "I saw that as a privilege and tried not to abuse it."

This student, now a senior, had other insights that reflected her own individual maturity. "You know, the number of candles on the cake may increase, but that doesn't necessarily mean you're mature," she said. "Maturity," she added, "is something others can see by the way you behave." For her, living on her own at a boarding school seemed to be the real catalyst for becoming an adult. She said, "I know I'm ready to move on to a bigger place." She has outgrown us, I thought, and that was our goal all along.

To nurture a girl from sixteen to twenty-five takes more than designer dresses and black-tie parties. Growing up is done in relationship with wise parents and committed teachers who stay involved and who know when to step back.

Tips & Tactics

Ask yourself how your daughter's responsibilities have increased now that she is a teenager. What is she now doing for herself that you used to do? If the list turns out to be short, sit down with her and talk about your desire to step back. See what she would suggest for how she can take more ownership for her life. Your signaling to her that it is time to do that also communicates to her that you know she is ready.

53. The Perils of Popularity
Implications of Belonging

By the time I was ready to go to South Junior High School, I knew that I wasn't part of the in group. Even if there had been a *How to Be Popular for Dummies*, I couldn't have made the turn on the road to being cool. I knew there were guys around, but to be popular you needed to be much more comfortable with them than I was. Then there was the look—I was off by a mile. I was still chubby, my face (adorned with acne) hadn't quite caught up with the size of my teeth, and I wore glasses.

By high school, I had thinned out and discovered contact lenses, but my orbit was still not within the constellation of the überpopular. Fortunately, the stakes were not so high in the sixties in my baby-boomer-filled school. Being popular meant that you navigated socially with more ease than others, but it didn't mean you had more power. Fitting in and being noticed, regardless of where you were on the social scaffolding, was within the grasp of most students. There were many places for membership—the musicians (my group), the nerds (also my group), ROTC (boys only), athletes (boys only), and thespians. As far as my parents were concerned, there was no cachet in my being a social diva, nor did they need me to be popular to enhance their social standing.

Times have changed. Today, the stakes are high for teens when it comes to being able to fit in. In *Odd Girl Out: The Hidden Culture of Aggression in Girls*, author Rachel Simmons discusses what we all know regarding the social land mines in the teen culture. Popular girls have access to "the booty of womanhood . . . makeup and boys . . . and parents born without genes for party supervision."[229] Less well understood, she goes on to say, is the role of friendships—the right number and the right ones—in a girl's social standing. For those girls in hot pursuit of sustaining their popularity, friendship becomes "a ticket [or] tool."[230] On the other end of the continuum, girls desperately seeking acceptance are at great risk for becoming pawns and exchanging their integrity for an invitation from those with social power. It is in settings where adults allow this "merciless competition for relationships" to go unchecked that there are winners and losers and that a girl's very sense of worth can be challenged so severely that it takes years for her to regain her equilibrium.[231]

Research now suggests that there are also long-term negative implications for teens who belong to Club Popularity. A longitudinal study of teen culture reveals that teens who are popular are so, according to researcher Joseph Allen, "in part because they are carefully attuned to the norms of their peer group."[232] He goes on to explain that "as these norms increasingly come to support even minor levels of deviant behavior during adolescence, popular teens may be particularly susceptible."[233] Specifically, according to Allen, the most socially skilled students are "three times as likely to be drinking by age 14 as those outside the group."[234]

Allen's work also suggests to me that parents may inadvertently play a role in shifting the norms of the teen culture. His findings reveal that popular adolescents not only navigate well in social interactions with their peer groups but also demonstrate a high level of social skill in dealing with adults, including their parents.[235] Teens' social charms, therefore, may cause us as parents to accede to adolescent demands and allow our teenage girls to have access to adult situations and environments long before they are ready, thus increasing their vulnerability to behaviors that carry risk.

At Miss Hall's School, we are committed to providing a setting for girls in which there are no in or out groups and where the peer-culture's norms are wholesome and its values intact. Preparing for college (and life) is difficult enough without a girl feeling either that she's on the outskirts or that she has to keep pace on the social treadmill. One girl described it this way: "[It's] being known for your ideas and your interests as well as the high level of respect in the culture that make the difference." Another girl agreed and noted, "We each have our own group of friends, but we all work with each other." What is key, she added, is that "we learn to listen to what others are saying and to approach others with an open mind."

Girls feel this way because we all work hard to sustain the culture they describe; we are all vigilant and respond when things go amiss. What is foremost in our minds as teachers, however, is sustaining a learning environment in which girls come to know that the source of their power is not in what they have or whom they know. It is in the clarity they develop about what they believe in deeply and in the sure knowledge that the world is waiting for their contributions.

Tips & Tactics

Pay attention to the friendships your daughter develops. Are you comfortable with her choices? When your daughter talks about her friends, listen for inconsistencies between what she describes and what you observe. Be aware that our own daughters can be experts in telling us what they know we want to hear. Always be open to the idea that your daughter may not yet be able to align her actions with her words. Trust her, and confirm that she is reporting accurately.

54. The Need to Belong
Adolescent Struggles, Societal Pressures

Is there an adult alive who does not remember being humiliated as a teenager? My mind goes immediately to seventh-grade gym class, where we girls were putting on our one-piece uniforms. We had all learned how to contort our bodies in such a way that, with arms free and using our Peter Pan-collared blouses as tents, we could manage a complete change of clothes without revealing any naked body parts. As we scurried out onto the auditorium stage to go through our thirty-minute drill, a petite, blond girl yelled out, "How ya doin', fatty?" Another flashback takes me to eighth grade, when I showed up at a boy-girl party proudly wearing a new dress. To my horror, every other girl had on the newest craze, Bermuda shorts.

Feeling unaccepted and isolated is normal in the teen years because it is during this time that a girl can lose track of who she is. One aspect of a girl's developmental process is the loss of middle-school identity. In most cases, she will have formed a very clear idea of herself in middle school. As she makes the transition to a more advanced curriculum, shifts into a higher cognitive area with more abstract thinking required, develops physically, deals with emerging sexual energy, interacts with more people, and loses old friends, she can feel fragile and miss the more confident girl she used to be. As a result, a girl acts one day as if she were twenty-four years old and the next as if she were twelve.

This chameleon existence can be confusing to an adolescent's peers, and it is not surprising that friendships might suffer and that a girl might feel excluded. Sociologist Barbara Schneider found that loneliness tops the list of issues that worry teenagers.[236] Her work with seven thousand adolescents also confirms what we know about the frequency with which girls change friendships in these years. Almost three-quarters of the closest friends named by seniors in her study were not even mentioned during the sophomore year.[237] My observations at the Miss Hall's School annual senior dinner, an evening of good-byes that occurs in the final week of the senior year, match Schneider's findings. By the time a girl is a junior, she is better able to settle into the kind of friendships that will last a lifetime because she is becoming confident in her unique self.

Another reason girls struggle with issues of membership has to do with the heightened self-awareness that is the trademark of adolescence. There is nothing new about teenagers being self-conscious about their appearance; that has been the case for generations. What has changed, however, is society's response over the past century to that preoccupation.[238] Instead of telling girls that it is the quality of their characters that matter, as dozens of alumnae heard Mira Hall say, or giving our daughters the message that pretty is as pretty does, as my mother said to me, we as a culture instead encourage girls' anxieties. Through a multibillion-dollar advertising industry, we tell our daughters that it is what they wear, how they look, and what they drive that guarantee acceptance. As a society, we have raised the stakes so high for what it takes to fit in that it's no wonder lots of girls feel left out.

Writer Stephen Hall has pointed out that our daughters are not alone in feeling insecure and worried about image. As Barbie has become thinner over the past several decades, G.I. Joe has bulked up.[239] Both girls and boys are at risk for abusing their bodies, whether through dieting or steroid use, in an attempt to reach the unattainable perfection that brings with it acceptance.

As adults, we are not going to eliminate the adolescent's struggle for identity and belonging because that struggle is a natural part of the maturation process. In addition, I do not believe that we are going to have any serious impact on corporate marketing plans targeting the lucrative teenage market.

However, there are things we can do. First, girls need adults around, even more than they will admit. Second, we must acknowledge how hard the struggle for acceptance is for adolescents and support them in their work. Being available to talk, helping a girl resist the messages of the mass media, and reminding her that lasting acceptance is based on the quality of her spirit are some of the most important means of support that we can give. Finally, it is our job as parents and educators to keep the adolescent culture in check and not to allow teenagers to make their own rules about who is in and who is out.

One of the reasons I like heading a boarding school is that there is time to pay attention to all the lessons girls need to learn. Thirty-five years from now when our current students reflect on their teen years, they may remember showing up in the wrong garb for the party. What I want them also to remember is that tolerance, compassion, and acceptance were everyday priorities.

Tips & Tactics

Pay attention to what you highlight when you are praising your daughter. Telling her she looks great in a new outfit is fine, but let her also hear your praise for an interesting perspective or the mature way she solved a problem.

55. Old-Fashioned Girls
Growing Up in Public

The kindergarten graduation at Washington Elementary School was under way on a warm May evening in my Missouri hometown. My five-year-old friends and I stood on the stage in our little white academic gowns and mortar boards, basking in the admiration of a room full of parents. As I stepped out to accept my diploma, I must have caught one of my Mary Janes on the hem of my gown. Suddenly, all of the snaps holding it together flew apart, and I found myself standing there in nothing but my Carter's underwear. Had I been five in the electronic age instead of several decades ago, my embarrassing moment would undoubtedly have been replayed all over the Internet instead of just in my mother's memory.

Thank heaven we were still in the electronic dark ages when I was growing up! Those of my generation can take some comfort in knowing that the junior-high confessions we wrote in dime-store diaries have long ago been discarded or packed away and that, in general, our youthful missteps and indiscretions were not available for all to see. We were able to prepare for adulthood with some privacy, and we didn't have to worry about our errors and excesses being recorded for posterity.

On the other hand, as Jeffrey Zaslow has pointed out in the *Wall Street Journal,* "Today's kids will enter adulthood with far more of their lives in plain view," thanks to social-networking sites, Internet blogs, and surveillance cameras.[240] He quotes a consultant who works with businesses to research prospective employees as saying, "Tell your kids to think of the Internet as a public stage that'll still be playing their show 20 years from now."[241]

Maintaining some privacy may be more important than we realize. We need time and a secure inner place in order to forge our lives. To become functioning individuals, our daughters must do what we have all had to do—take our essential problems inside ourselves and assume responsibility. The danger for a girl in sharing her predicaments on the web where everyone knows everything is not embarrassment alone, but the eroding of her personal boundaries. Instead of developing a distinct inner core, she can become diffuse and vulnerable to influences that she would otherwise discard.

There is another unintended consequence of so many making so much public. It turns out that our worst characteristics, the ones we once had the luxury of examining and discarding, are now widely available for imitation in this voyeur culture we have created. By sharing and baring all, we generate epidemics of bad behavior, as public displays are imitated endlessly by people who haven't yet developed the self-discipline required to live honorably. Our public discourse, therefore, has changed from calm, reasoned debate to a contest of who can shout loudest and be the most insulting. Any teen girl with access to the Internet has a front row seat from which to view this behavior.

One example of unbecoming conduct is discussed in the *New York Times* article "American Awful," which describes the television program *American Idol* as "a series of vicious encounters between hopeful but pathetically untalented young people and celebrity judges being paid to make fun of them."[242] According to the *Times* article, some contestants seem to have been advanced to the level of appearing on the show not because they can sing but because they are "poor, of low intelligence or even mildly disturbed."[243] These contestants hope to move forward, only to be ridiculed and demeaned by adults who should know better.

The erosion of basic civility is everywhere. Our daughters do not have to look very far to see people being watched, humiliated, and degraded. But what they don't see often enough is society's disdain in response. Those who bullied and harassed used to be shunned; now they are applauded on national TV. Society's response to inappropriate behavior has changed dramatically, making it harder to teach girls to respect others as well as themselves.

Sustaining an atmosphere of respect is essential in order for girls to take risks, to discover who they are, and to discard the parts of themselves they don't like or that don't work. With the help of mature, understanding adults, girls grow up the old-fashioned way, according to their own strength and better selves.

Tips & Tactics

It is your choice as a parent whether or not you allow your daughter to participate in social-networking sites. Just because "everyone is doing it" doesn't mean she must. What is clear, however, is that teen Internet use must be monitored. In partnership with your daughter, set boundaries and rules about how you expect her to conduct herself and what the consequences will be if she missteps. A teen girl is still developing her ability to anticipate the long-term implications of her actions. This ultimately requires a parent to be clear about expectations and vigilant in monitoring compliance.

56. No Proof Needed
Overcoming Cultural Stereotypes

When my daughter Emily knew that I was going to be in Texas combining business with a visit with her, she suggested we see some live theater. The choices were *Proof*, by David Auburn, which I had seen before, and Claudia Shear's *Dirty Blond*, a show about Mae West. I opted for a repeat of *Proof*. Because I was the one traveling, Emily conceded, provided that the play was preceded by dinner at her favorite Moroccan restaurant.

Proof takes place at the University of Chicago and is about Catherine, the twenty-five-year-old daughter of a famous mathematician. She has suspended her education to care for her father, who after a brilliant early career has sunk into serious mental illness. When he unexpectedly dies, a graduate student named Hal discovers a ground-breaking manuscript among the mathematician's nonsense-filled notebooks. Hal is enthusiastic about what he thinks is the great mathematician's last work, but eventually Catherine tells him that she has written the proof. Neither Hal nor Catherine's sister believes her.

Catherine explains her ability to do this complex work by saying that she has lived with and learned from her father her entire life. The audience learns that there are precious few women doing high-level mathematics, none without advanced degrees. Catherine's writing of the proof, therefore, seems to Hal unlikely and verging on impossible. However, after a great struggle Hal gives in, acknowledges Catherine's work, and sits down to read the proof with her.

Following this second viewing of the play, I considered its themes. First, Catherine was caught between her love for and devotion to her father and her desire to attend college. Second, she learned mathematics brilliantly and creatively but in an unorthodox style. She hadn't finished the curriculum and gotten the professional seal of approval, so how could she produce great work? Third, she was a woman trying to work in a male bastion and as a result suffered doubt, dismissiveness, and obstacles. It was a compelling picture of the struggles of a young woman whose talent is in the field of mathematics.

A few years ago, a study at one of the leading women's colleges found that if a young woman is not already thinking about a career in the sciences by the time she arrives at college for her freshman year, there is little hope that she will move in that direction during her undergraduate years.[244] That stunning finding contributed to our decision here at Miss Hall's School to redouble our efforts to encourage every girl to stick with math and science for the full four years of high school. One initiative we undertook was to adopt a physics-first science curriculum. Before the program was launched in 1998, 43 percent of our students took four years of science. Largely due to introducing physics to our ninth-grade girls, that percentage zoomed to 74 percent over the next decade.

A *Discover* magazine article by Peggy Orenstein about women in science presents sobering information and confirms that it will take more than solid preparation in the sciences to turn the professional tide.[245] Nobel Prize nominee and renowned biologist Elizabeth Blackburn, on whom the article focuses, says that she used to subscribe to the pipeline theory: encourage women early, and the gender gap in science-related fields will disappear. "But," she says, "the pipeline has been good for a number of years, and it hasn't taken care of the problem."[246]

Orenstein goes on to point out that there is still unintentional bias in higher education that is only made worse by the overlap of childbearing years and the tenure process.[247] Beyond that, Blackburn and others say they believe that many factors, from what is described as the combative language of science to the emphasis on self-promotion, put women scientists at odds with the science culture.[248] Blackburn also mentions something that I have noted and discussed with colleagues for years: even a woman's tone of voice is a factor in her being taken seriously or, as Blackburn explains it, in her work being accepted as authoritative.[249]

By any standard, Blackburn is a success in her field and credits her parents, both physicians, as well as her single-sex secondary school and college for allowing her to move beyond limited cultural stereotypes.[250] She also endorses the potent influence of strong mentors who encourage and validate.[251]

What most caught my eye in the article, however, was Blackburn's theory that instead of women adapting to science, science instead will have to adapt to women.[252] One of Blackburn's young protégées, a thirty-year-old postdoctoral student, personalized this concept by saying, "[I had to be] a person that I didn't want to be in order to be successful as a scientist."[253]

By the time a girl begins high school, she has begun to experience the tug-of-war that, if left unchecked, leads to her separating from who she really is. In *Reviving Ophelia: Saving the Selves of Adolescent Girls*, psychologist Mary Pipher describes it this way: "Adolescence is when girls experience social pressure to put aside their authentic selves and to display only a small portion of their gifts."[254] In other words, they are asked to submerge their talents and their ambitions and to settle for traditional support roles.

What we don't want for girls is for them to spend their time trying to be what they aren't. Our goal as parents and as educators is for them to be able to be who they are and for *that* to have value in the world. By listening to what girls say, giving them honest feedback, and encouraging their originality, we prepare them to insist that the world take them seriously as scientists and as people.

Tips & Tactics

A girl learns early what others want her to be, say, and do in order to be accepted. Look for signs that your daughter is losing track of who she is and what she values as she tries to please everyone around her. Ask her if there are times when she has remained silent and not expressed a thought she assumed others would not like. Ask her to describe a time when she spoke out and others did not agree. What happened? How did it make her feel?

57. Effortless Perfection
The Value of Self

Getting ready for school in the sixties was a grind. There was the makeup, the hose and garter belt, the white blouse that had been sprinkled and ironed, and then, the hair. I'd wash it in the evening, wrap it around huge brush rollers, and put a plastic drawstring bag, into which a tube of hot air flowed, over my hair. If I positioned my head just right, I could fall asleep in that contraption and have bunches of curls in the morning. Of course, they had to be mashed down, gotten under control, and then herded into a flip that just brushed the shoulders. At school, someone would say, "Your hair looks great!" To which I'd reply, "This mop? It just does this."

I don't know how perfect my appearance was, but making it seem effortlessly acquired was expected. It still is. Duke University implemented a number of initiatives in the past several years to address significant cultural ills in campus life. The problems were uncovered as part of the Women's Initiative, which was undertaken as a campuswide project to improve the campus experience for women at Duke. In a report about the progress of the program, Donna Lisker recalled the findings of the study, which described an expectation of "effortless perfection" for female students.[255] Women were to "look cute, be funny, be quiet," as one student said.[256] The women who participated in the study reported that they felt they must be "smart, accomplished, fit, beautiful, and popular," all without visible effort.[257]

At the heart of effortless perfection is the tradeoff girls and young women make when they abdicate control of their lives in service of meeting the requirements of others in a perfection-obsessed culture. What they sense, quite accurately, is that the textured, variegated authentic self poses a risk. It doesn't play well in academic settings such as college campuses and in some sectors of the real world.

One of those sectors is the workplace. A *New York Times* article referenced a study conducted by Catalyst, a leading research organization that focuses on women in business. In the study report, entitled *Damned If You Do, Doomed If You Don't*, findings from a survey of senior executives reveal that it is through a lens of gender stereotypes that women are typically viewed at work.[258] If they conduct themselves in stereotypical ways, which the report defines as focusing "on work relationships" and expressing "concern for other people's perspectives," they are perceived to be less competent than male leaders.[259] If they behave in ways that are viewed as traditionally male, such as being assertive, they are seen as "too tough" and "unfeminine."[260] In the same article, professor and author Joan Williams sums up the dilemma. As leaders, women have "to choose between being liked but not respected, or respected but not liked."[261] What a conundrum for young women who are trying to figure out how to succeed!

Here at Miss Hall's School, we believe that the key for schools and workplaces is to articulate intentionally a core value of authenticity. Once that is done, students and employees must be encouraged to discover and express their core selves. We have seen that when the school actively values authenticity, girls are inspired to penetrate layers of conditioning, habit, and expectation to find what they really think and believe. When they do this, the entire discourse of the school becomes settled, considered, and creative.

What must accompany the encouragement of individual authenticity, however, is the insistence on respect for diverse opinions and styles of expression and presentation. Even though the value of deep respect seems intuitively to be correct to most people, we find that it is essential to articulate it on a conceptual level. That is, it is helpful to adolescent girls if we are explicit about our shared values. In practice, of course, if individuals feel that they are respected by their school or workplace, they are more likely to respect others. As many studies have shown, what we know as the Golden Rule is a value held throughout the world: mutual respect is generated by our behaving toward others as we want them to behave toward us. This respect, when practiced broadly, has a profoundly cohesive effect on a community.

We see this strategy working every day here at the school. Girls know that they are developing their strongest, most authentic, and most honorable selves in a richly diverse setting. They nurture their capacity not to get caught up in biases and to see beyond stereotypes to engage with each other in meaningful work. We believe that these young women will have the courage and confidence to challenge the status quo and to work to right our topsy-turvy society that discourages broad participation in solving complex problems. It is these authentic activities that constitute effortless perfection.

Tips & Tactics

Talk to your daughter about the social dynamics at her school. Who are the popular girls? Why does your daughter believe they are popular? If she is part of the in group, ask her what personal qualities have allowed her to have membership. If she is not in the popular echelon, what does she know about the reasons she is excluded? By asking your daughter to share her perceptions, you are guiding her to distinguish between fleeting and enduring values.

58. Imperfect Perfection
Shaping a Satisfying Life

When I was in high school, the idea of building a college-ready transcript never occurred to me. I joined clubs when I was interested. I would have joined an athletic team, but sports for girls had not yet made it to Joplin Senior High School. My friends and I earned good grades, and we took what today would be the equivalent of honors courses, because why would we not? After graduation, many top students attended the local junior college for their freshman year before transferring to midwestern colleges and universities. Compared with today's teen's full-boil, high-intensity experience of doing it all and doing it all perfectly, my high-school career was a gentle simmer.

New York Times reporter Sara Rimer has described the lives of adolescent girls attending the highly competitive Newton (Massachusetts) North High School, where "girls . . . do everything: Varsity sports. Student government. Theater. Community service."[262] Yet despite this achievement, "being an amazing girl often doesn't feel like enough . . . with all the other amazing girls" in evidence.[263] Rimer describes the pressure girls feel to measure up in our name-brand American culture and to achieve all the top spots while still being oneself, being cool, and as one girl described it, being "effortlessly hot."[264] Rimer sums it up by saying, "What it comes down to . . . is that the eternal adolescent search for self is going on at the same time as the quest for the perfect resume."[265]

With that kind of pressure on today's seventeen-year-olds, it's no wonder many first-year college students are exhausted before the college academic year has even begun. Perhaps as a result, a relatively new field of study, positive psychology, is gaining a following in many US colleges. According to *New York Times* reporter D. T. Max, positive psychology focuses on "optimism, gratitude, mindfulness, hope, spirituality," all essential values when it comes to shaping a life.[266] Max says that this new brand of psychology "is not only about maximizing personal happiness but also about embracing civic engagement and spiritual connectedness, hope and charity."[267] The idea is that one identifies one's "signature strengths" and then uses them to lead an honorable life.[268]

Combining the concepts of positive psychology with a traditional, college-preparatory curriculum is beginning to interest secondary-school educators in the United States and abroad. In a general way, however, Miss Hall's School has historically integrated the values of this new science into its approach to educating girls as a way to enhance meaning and relevance for our students. Academic and intellectual growth is, of course, the foundation, and it turns out that education itself is one of the documented indicators of a fulfilling life. George Vaillant, a proponent of positive psychology, directed a longitudinal study at Harvard University on well-being and successful aging. Among the study's findings was that "education trumps money and social prestige as a route to health and happiness."[269] As we educate our students at Miss Hall's School, our goal is to create a learning environment that propels a girl forward to desire more education, not one that exhausts her resources.

Within the context of such a productive learning environment, we encourage our students and our daughters to be optimistic as they come to trust that they are in charge of creating options and making choices. Each girl learns to be hopeful as she hones the skills needed to persevere through difficulty. She matures with confidence as she is guided to seek purpose, not perfection. In a connection-rich setting, she becomes enterprising and bold as she is set free by the knowledge that life is not a zero-sum game. No one has to lose for her to gain.

It is also in this type of environment that gratitude is continuously held up so that a girl will develop a deep appreciation for the interconnectedness she has with others. In letters of congratulations to students who earn academic honors, I often ask, "Who helped you to achieve this goal?" As girls write in the journals required for Horizons, the school's community-service, experiential-learning program, they are prompted to answer the question, "What gifts did you receive today at your Horizons site?"

A deep level of civic engagement lifts a girl to a higher plane, one that gives her a vision for the future because of the change she is making now. Trying to be perfect pales in comparison with knowing you are making a difference.

Tips & Tactics

When a girl is encouraged to think about expansive long-term goals, she is better able to resist the narrower goal of short-term perfection. If your daughter is overly focused on making the honor roll, ask her to describe why that is important. Keep asking why until she is able to respond with a comment that indicates how she would like to have influence in the world. That will open the door for more conversations about the many roads that can lead her to where she would eventually like to be.

59. The Art of the Possible
Erasing the Fear of Failure

"You make the piano talk," is what people would tell me after a church performance or a recital when I was young. I heard it enough in the early years of my music study that I started to believe it myself. My parents added their support. At a time when the family budget couldn't easily accommodate lessons and a piano, Mom and Dad found a way to provide both.

There was emotional support as well. Mom would sit on the piano bench with me, bolstering my confidence through the tediousness of learning a new piece. (She also provided incentive for me to practice by suggesting that she clean up after dinner while I played through my lesson.) Dad did his part by stopping by the music store on Fridays after work and bringing home the sheet music for the newest *Your Hit Parade* tune. I played while he sang, and so I learned to sight-read.

I felt no pressure from my parents to play well or even to play at all. It was all about having an opportunity to see what was possible. Therefore, I was free to run with my talent and great love of music as far as I wanted to go, which, as it turned out, was through two college degrees and a twenty-five-year career in performing and teaching.

Times have changed. Our daughters live in a world where life feels more like a fiercely competitive game in which the fear of failure is constant. There is enormous pressure to measure up. If you can't be number one, you must at least be in the top ten. No wonder we're all anxious. Now imagine being a teen in this high-stakes climate. When failure is not an option, how can a girl live in the realm of possibility?

Ben Zander, conductor of the Boston Philharmonic Orchestra, writes in his book *The Art of Possibility: Transforming Professional and Personal Life* about dealing unsuccessfully for decades with his New England Conservatory students' fear of failure. He writes, "Class after class, the students would be in such a chronic state of anxiety over the measurement of their performance that they would be reluctant to take risks with their playing."[270] Knowing that this was a serious obstacle to their becoming great performers, he gave them all an A, the only grade that would "put them at ease."[271] There was a requirement, however: each student had to write a letter to him, dated the last day of the term, reflecting on why the A was deserved.

This exercise interested me, so on a cold, snowy Friday night in early December, I found two Miss Hall's School students (a freshwoman and a sophomore) with time on their hands who agreed to meet me in my office. I told the girls that I wanted them to think of their hardest class, imagine it being June, and picture receiving an A in the course. Handing out paper and pen, I then asked each girl to write to her teacher, completing the sentence, "I received the A because . . ." The girls also were asked to describe how they would have felt after receiving this high mark and how their attitude toward the course might have changed.

"I stepped up to the plate and challenged myself. I welcomed new projects with open arms and set long-term goals," wrote one girl. "I have become a relieved person. I have worked hard and am so proud," wrote the other. After the writing assignment, the girls and I chatted, and phrases like "changed my whole perspective" and "seeing the bigger picture" came up. In other words, the girls were thinking about what was possible, not whether or not they measured up.

Zander is not suggesting that standards don't matter. His conservatory students must play with precision and musicality. However, his philosophy, and one we share here at the school, is that our relationships with students need to be based on much more than how well girls meet a set of standards. The exercise of "giving the A," whether literally or figuratively, allows the teacher, writes Zander, "to line up with her students in their efforts to produce the outcome, rather than lining up with the standards against these students."[272] In our educational philosophy, we line up with our students by helping each girl to own her learning and to draw from that sense of ownership the realization that she is competent and able. The confidence she feels will propel her forward to desire more, to take risks, to stretch, and to achieve at the highest levels. In other words, our work is to allow girls to live and think in the realm of possibility.

Tips & Tactics

When your daughter faces a challenge, ask her to do the following:

Describe what she would see as a successful outcome ("I want to make the varsity team.")

Pretend she has achieved at that level ("I made the varsity team!")

Describe what she did to meet her goal ("I added an hour to my practice time for three weeks before tryouts.")

Tell you how she feels about this achievement ("I feel proud to know I made this happen for myself.")

By teaching your daughter to reflect on what she desires and to envision success, you inspire her to believe that she can act on her own behalf and affect outcomes.

60. Popping Back
Resilience in the Face of Challenge

I was a freshman in college when I agreed to accompany a tenor soloist who was giving his final performance before graduating. There was a lot of music to execute, and I was also to perform all three movements of Bach's *Italian Concerto* midpoint in the recital. Everything went smoothly until about two minutes into my solo performance, when I suffered a total train wreck. Memory failed, not once, not twice, but several times. Each time, I started over, only to stall out again. The silence from the audience sounded like heavy machinery to my ears. My face burned with embarrassment. I was flushed, hot, and sick to my stomach. I went into automatic-pilot mode, regained my footing, and completed all of the movements.

To this day, I don't know how I managed to remain on the stage. Some sort of inner stamina, no doubt related to my distaste for total humiliation, allowed me to stay put and cope. Nor did this experience discourage me in my desire to be a musician. I went on to earn two music degrees and negotiated, with some measure of success, hundreds of performances over the years.

Resilience, that ability to manage regardless of the challenge and to bounce back, is a good thing. If we could purchase our daughters' life skills from a catalogue, we'd no doubt put in a double order of resilience.

Our hearts sink when a daughter collapses because no one will sit with her at lunch or because she fails a quiz. We feel her pain. And just as we protected her by putting childproof locks on the kitchen cabinets when she was two, our first reaction when she faces difficulty as a teen is to protect her again by becoming her shield and defender. But we can't sweep up all the gravel in the world. Our adolescents need to skin their knees and learn that they can brush themselves off and move on.

Teaching resilience is a challenge. In their book *Raising Resilient Children: Fostering Strength, Hope, and Optimism in Your Child,* child psychologists Robert Brooks and Sam Goldstein say that no parent would argue about the goal of instilling resilience in youngsters, but "knowing what needs to be done is not the same as knowing how to do it."[273] They see thousands of families in their clinical practices and report that otherwise well-meaning and loving parents "either do not understand the parental practices that contribute to raising a resilient child or do not use what they know."[274]

There is a large body of research on resilience and on what factors contribute to some individuals being able to respond effectively to stressful circumstances.[275] From this research, we have become more enlightened regarding how we can create what psychologist Elizabeth Debold describes as "relational hardiness zones—a context in which girls can experience greater control, commitment, and challenge."[276] The central idea is that girls must "perceive connection and the commitment of adults," and that perception is created when we as adults can master the art of really listening to our daughters.[277] When we hear what girls are saying and encourage them to speak openly about what is on their minds, we validate their feelings and their experiences. The implicit message in the hundreds of conversations that we, as parents and educators, have every day with adolescents needs to be that we take them and their ideas seriously. When girls are convinced that their thinking is valuable, they develop a solid core that can always be accessed. Without a reliable, secure center, no resilience is possible.

Finding ways for girls to develop a sense of purpose and providing them with opportunities to experience effective action are other powerful factors in building resilience. Hardiness zones are not, says Debold "precious spaces in which girls bond through suffering but spaces in which their personal experiences can be understood . . . and in which they can develop skills through being involved in making change within their communities."[278] It is essential that we provide learning environments in which a girl can have influence and thus come to believe in her ability to be an effective leader.

We also encourage resilience in girls by challenging them to set and achieve goals. The competence they feel when they are successful allows us to talk with them specifically about the unique talents that made their achievements possible. Even highly accomplished girls are all too ready to attribute academic success to luck instead of to intellectual strength and solid effort. Adolescent girls need to believe in themselves and to be aware of their strong abilities in order to recognize their own value. With this recognition, they can always recover from even the most embarrassing train wrecks.

We know that resilient people don't handle everything alone. Some years ago, the cover story in *Psychology Today* reported that one of the standout findings of research into resiliency is that people who cope well "are able to ask for help or recruit others to help them."[279] Just as teenagers do not benefit when we overprotect, they also lose out when we troubleshoot their problems. Our job as teachers and parents is to guide girls in learning how to access the help they need and to develop the patience required to let them grow strong on their own.

We don't know what lies ahead for our young women. We can't build walls around them and eliminate danger from the world. The most we can do is instill in them unstinting hope and courage and a bedrock competency to face the adversity life brings their way.

Tips & Tactics

Look for ways to encourage a sense of agency in your daughter. Is there a family project (planning a vacation or researching fuel efficiency for an automobile purchase) for which she could assume responsibility, in full or in part? Instead of your making rules for Internet use, ask your daughter to create a first draft for your review.

61. The Pursuit of Happiness
What We Wish for Our Daughters

The tiny orange-juice shop in my hometown had the coldest, sweetest orange juice, always freshly squeezed. I loved going there with my grandmom or, as she said, being "blown in" by a large gust of wind that always caught us by surprise as we rounded the corner onto Main Street. To me at four years old, that was happiness, as was a fresh box of Crayola crayons, a cold lime Popsicle, and my dad coming home from work.

Happiness isn't always that easy to find but is something that most Americans, including our country's founders, believe is worth pursuing. However, some commentators think that the quest is out of control. In the *Forbes* magazine article "The Pursuit of Emptiness: Why Americans Have Never Been a Happy Bunch," John Perry Barlow says that while few Americans actually seem to be happy, they believe they are entitled, even obliged, to find happiness.[280] This endless search, he says, produces a "monstrous, insatiable hunger" that leads us more often than not to overconsumption.[281]

Didn't our mothers tell us that we can't buy happiness? Much of our culture weighs in on the other side. Madison Avenue spends lots of money so that teenage girls will spend even more on stuff to make them smile. Confronted with so much hype and glitz, it is easy for girls to be seduced. But I wonder if we, as parents and educators, don't also oversimplify and oversell happiness. By not taking the time to talk about what it truly means to be happy, we create a goal that is as elusive as the digitally altered look of a fashion model.

In *The Difference: Growing Up Female in America*, author Judy Mann says that even after the changes brought on by the women's movement, researchers still find that when parents are asked what they want for their early-teenage daughters, they respond that they want their girls to be happy. In contrast, parents of boys reply to the same question with a specific occupation. According to the researchers, "It may be easier to become a doctor than to be happy. We may be setting up something more unrealistic and unobtainable for girls than what we expect for boys."[282]

On the other hand, identifying happiness with occupation may be just another way that parents avoid the issue of defining happiness. If we refuse to equate happiness with pleasure and gratification, if we even refuse to equate it with status or power, then we are forced to dig deeper. The great religious traditions insist that the goal of living is to bring our thoughts and actions into harmony with enduring values and spiritual truths. If this is indeed our goal for ourselves and for our children, we must take charge of our lives and move in the direction we know is right.

Sadly, the search for enduring value and the happiness it brings can, like the search for happiness through objects, be dizzying. There are many purveyors of the right virtue and the right way, each selling a particular version of happiness or salvation. In helping our daughters realize a sturdier and more stable fulfillment, we emphasize the search for each girl's authentic self. In other words, we ask each girl to continually consult her inner compass. What is the deepest voice—not the frantic surface desire—whispering? We know that when girls grow confident in what they most deeply know, they will be independent, strong, and moral.

In *How Girls Thrive: An Essential Guide for Educators (and Parents)*, JoAnn Deak says that girls need the three Cs of competence, confidence, and connectedness to develop high self-esteem.[283] Here at Miss Hall's School, we have overlaid activities that build competency and skill onto an authentic foundation. The strength of girls who have accomplished this growth in turn lets us help them cultivate a sense of purpose and higher calling. We applaud real achievement, listen to girls' ideas, affirm their unique strengths, and ask how they plan to make a difference for good in the world.

In a connected environment, the critical foundation for a girl's development is laid. She will pursue her dreams as well as her happiness, not in a frenzied attempt to indulge every whim, but in an ongoing process of acquiring the skills she will need to be self-sufficient and dedicated in the world.

Tips & Tactics

Ask your daughter to make a list of what made her happy when she was much younger. Then, ask her to make a list of what makes her happy now. How have the happiness factors changed? Are there indications in your daughter's current list that being self-reliant is part of her happiness? If so, help her to see that connection. Perhaps her involvement in helping others is part of her list. If so, ask her to identify the personal qualities she brings to her work with others in need.

62. Sweet Corn and Tomatoes
Intentional Reflection in a Hurried World

In late summer, when the corn got as high as an elephant's eye, my mom, my brother, Mom's friend Ruthie, and I would drive up to Dedrick, Missouri, where Ruthie's dad, Mr. Key, lived on a farm. He grew tomatoes and corn, and when we'd arrive in time for lunch, there would be an enormous pot on the stove, full of water. "We'll get this boiling," Mr. Key would say, "then you kids run out to the field and get the corn." Tom and I said we could go right then, but Mr. Key said, "No, the water has to be boiling." When that moment came, we, the "runners," flew out to the field, got one ear for each person, and raced back. Mr. Key whisked off the husks and slid the corn into the pot. It cooked quickly, and we all sat down with the corn and a large platter of just-picked tomatoes and ate. When we had each finished the first batch, we repeated the process—Mr. Key started the water boiling, and Tom and I raced to the field to pick another round. As I recall, we each ate a dozen ears every time we went to see Mr. Key in the late summer.

I thought about those visits often when I was young. It intrigued me that there was a precision to the ritual of picking and cooking corn, that by being intentional one could eat corn at precisely its peak of flavor, before any sugar had the chance to convert to starch. There was time to reflect on such things when I was ten. My brain was not interrupted by a text message or a tweet. It was not fragmented into minireceptors for ear plugs, hardware platforms, and plasma screens. In the quiet stretches that linked the simple routines of daily life in the fifties, I had the time to reflect on my experiences and on myself, and I was able to make meaning out of those reflections.

Girls still need time to think and reflect as they grow up. Psychologist Jane M. Healy reminds us in *Endangered Minds: Why Children Don't Think—and What We Can Do about It* that for children to be prepared even for the intellectual demands of reading, "minds must be trained to use language, to *reflect*, and to persist in solving problems."[284] By the time a girl is a teen, she is about the business of shaping a personal identity, using what she is learning through her experiences to inform the choices she will make about who she wants to be and what matters most to her. Psychologist David Elkind writes in *The Hurried Child: Growing Up Too Fast Too Soon* that for adolescents to do this work, they need "consistent experiences of self," a "consistent sense . . . of their relations to adults and to the peer group."[285] When those experiences are missing or when the information they are gathering is "inconsistent and discrepant," he adds, "a sense of personal identity can be severely inhibited."[286]

How can the information our daughters are receiving every day not be inconsistent and discrepant with the barrage of sound bites, myriad transmitters, and constant interruptions? Moreover, how can girls find the time to draw meaning from their experiences when so much time is spent whizzing through their actual and virtual worlds? And when the time to reflect on herself and her experiences is not sufficient, how is a girl supposed to develop a reliable sense of her real self, understand her strengths, and discover where she is vulnerable?

Interventions that give girls opportunities to do this important work are precious and essential. Every year one of our English teachers here at Miss Hall's School assigns "This I Believe" essays to her students as an approach to the study of *Hamlet*.[287] The challenge to each girl is to step out of her comfort zone and take the healthy risk of engaging with her reality using her authentic voice. It is a risk for a girl to assert what she believes when the subject matter must have a connection to her core values and beliefs. As our English teacher noted, "Girls have to go to another realm to reveal what most deeply matters."

Here at the school, we set aside time in our community-service, experiential-learning program for girls to reflect formally on their off-campus projects. In small faculty-led groups, students confront questions about the purpose, social implications, challenges, and rewards of the work they are doing. The goal of these conversations is to stir a girl's interest in continuing to reflect upon the greater personal meaning of these experiences. Over time, it is through reflection that she will create the vivid image of her unique, powerful, and authentic self, though perhaps without the immediate reward of sweet Missouri corn and tomatoes.

Tips & Tactics

Create time in your family's schedule when your daughter is not permitted to engage electronically. Whether it is the evening family dinner (sans electronic devices), an hour-before-bed quiet reading time, a knee-to-knee check-in with your daughter twice a week, or an unplugged weekend once a month, find times that allow you to strengthen your connection to each other and that provide her with time to be alone with her thoughts.

PART FOUR:

Teaching with Purpose

63. Rethinking Happily Ever After
Facing Life Head-On

When I first took the job as head of Miss Hall's School and staff members came to me with a question or problem, my initial thought was, we'll let the head of school deal with that. Then I would remember that I was the head. One is often tempted to look around for someone else to make tough decisions. Even as parents, or maybe especially as parents, we would like to be rescued from having to deal with the hard stuff our children bring to us. But as adults, we know that there is usually no one else to shift our problems to, so we must be self-reliant and face life head-on.

Teaching girls how to face life head-on and be in charge of their lives is a standard curriculum topic for the adolescent years. There is an extra cultural factor involved for girls, however, because much in the media-driven culture still promotes the notion that being female means being helpless. Young girls are taught early to identify with princesses waiting for a rescue from Prince Charming, as the shelves of many toy stores will confirm. Weakness and dependency are qualities a teen girl will see vastly overrepresented by females in television sitcoms, video games, and movies. Even the Internet serves up long lists of bridal shops, shoe stores, beauty pageants, and dance studios with "Cinderella" in their business names.

The antidote for helplessness, we have found, is to put girls in charge. One of our strategies at Miss Hall's School is to communicate to students that we depend on them to lead class meetings and sports teams, to sit on committees, to take charge of special events, to produce school publications, and to represent the school through various off-campus programs. Girls also learn here that they are in charge of making their dreams come true. Setting goals and knowing how to move steadily toward them require a girl to learn and practice skills. We teach girls how to manage their time; we do not manage it for them. We teach girls how to advocate for what they need; we do not advocate on their behalf. In other words, we teach young women what they will be required to know and we cheer from the sidelines, but we do not run their race. As Women's Basketball Hall of Fame inductee and girls basketball coach Dorothy Gaters has said, "We control our own destiny. . . . At some point we need to step up and take control."[288]

The temptation to look around for someone else to do the difficult work of being in charge is tempting for girls, because taking action to control one's destiny involves taking risks, and that includes the risk of failure. In a *New York Times* article describing the reasons women have not come as far in such arenas as business and politics as might have been predicted twenty-five years ago, author Joanne Lipman writes that progress has been too narrowly defined by numbers (for example, the number of women rising to the top of their fields).[289] Instead, according to Lipman, progress should be defined by the degree to which attitudes are changing. Specifically, she writes, those attitudes "have taken a giant leap backward."[290] Women need to learn "to take risks," she says, and adds that this is a challenge for women "brought up in a culture that celebrates unrealistic perfection in every sphere."[291]

As girls undertake the great work of becoming competent to lead their lives, they will be taking healthy risks and experiencing failure. Our job in supporting them is to teach them how to plan for and recover quickly from setbacks. I like what social media and technology expert Charlene Li says about failure in her book *Open Leadership: How Social Technology Can Transform the Way You Lead*. Although she is referring to companies, her advice applies to individuals and specifically to how we approach our work with girls. "The key," she writes, "is to make failure acceptable so that you're not afraid to fail."[292]

Girls learn at Miss Hall's School that falling short of the goal is an opportunity to identify an area that needs attention. Whether that means additional time in extra-help sessions with teachers or more practice shooting foul shots depends on the project. What failure is not about is the lessening of one's personal worth. When a girl comes to understand that distinction, she is free to embrace failure just as she embraces success. Leading change in a community, being in charge of one's life, knowing how to take healthy risks, and being skilled in recovering from setbacks are the competencies that will take a girl from "once upon a time" to "happily ever after."

Tips & Tactics

Examine the way you respond to failure. Our daughters are watching us, and we must attempt to model the behaviors we want them to adopt.

• • •

As your daughter grows through the teen years, be aware that a parent's role is to step back and let her develop and practice her problem-solving skills. Every time your instinct is to fix whatever is wrong in her life, pause and ask yourself, should my daughter be addressing this problem? If the answer is yes, coach her in how to get started.

64. In Her Element
Reaching for the Possible

For my first college voice lesson, I was assigned to a graduate teaching assistant. Walking into her studio, I felt confident as a singer and hopeful about the possibility of a singing career. Toward the end of the thirty-minute session and thinking about the specific emphasis for my music degree, I said to my instructor, "I'm still not sure where I want to put my major focus—voice, piano, or organ." Without hesitation, she replied, "You can focus on one of the last two; your major won't be voice." What a shock!

I had sung "O Holy Night" on Christmas Eve at my church, performed with two choral groups in high school, and crooned "The River Is Wide" and "Three Jolly Coachmen" with ukulele and friend to entertain my parents' dinner group. I had soloed in "How Betsy Ross Made the Flag" for the local women's club, and I had studied voice for three years. My parents, grandparents, and friends had told me that I had a beautiful voice. Clearly, what I had just heard from my college voice instructor would require an adjustment in thinking.

It did not take long for me to understand that the teaching assistant's assessment was spot-on. In my new setting, I began to hear other students who *were* voice majors, and I wondered what I could possibly have been thinking in considering a vocal major. I simply did not have the instrument that others had, and my teacher knew it.

In discussing his book *The Element: How Finding Your Passion Changes Everything*, author and consultant Ken Robinson told of his interview with Paul McCartney: "I asked if he had enjoyed music at school. He said he hated it. Nobody thought he had any musical talent."[293] Robinson went on to say that McCartney mentioned that George Harrison was also in the music class. McCartney told Robinson, "Nobody thought he had any talent either."[294] Robinson quipped, "So this one music teacher had half the Beatles in his class, and he missed it."[295]

If a teacher can make an accurate assessment of a student's potential, the student is free to recognize and develop the talent that she might otherwise have missed. As Robinson says, "Talent is buried deep and unless you look for it [and are] given the encouragement and conditions for it to flourish, you don't discover it."[296] It is essential that we help a young person discover her talent, because unless she does, according to Robinson, her ability to shape a fulfilling life is compromised.[297]

Most teachers would agree with Robinson that talent is often buried deep. It is easy to spot and applaud the math whiz, the star volleyball player, or the sensational actress. However, as educators we are looking for the talent and promise in *every* student and for the less obvious but no less potent qualities that make a girl who she is. An essential piece of our professional skill is recognizing a girl's exceptional facilities (for example, her particular flair and passion for creative solutions, her unusually well-defined sense of justice, or her distinct ability for simplifying complex topics), those vivid characteristics that will animate her life.

When we see where a student's passion and talent meet, it is our job as educators to help her see it too. We do that when we validate her opinion, remark on a brilliant insight, or encourage her challenging voice in a debate. We also allow her to see her unique talent when we call attention to abilities she may take for granted. Two senior leaders here at Miss Hall's School led the entire school community recently in Catch Phrase, a word-guessing game. With aplomb they organized over two hundred girls and adults into teams and runoff matches and had us all cheering wildly for those who survived to the semifinal round. They accomplished all this in a twenty-five-minute time slot. In applauding their success, we pointed out to these students that they demonstrated unusual ability to organize and execute a complex logistical task. The hope is that our response allowed them to recognize this ability.

Finally, girls will have far greater clarity about their authentic abilities when we give them, as my teacher gave me, realistic feedback. At Miss Hall's School, we are more thoughtful in shaping our remarks than my instructor was, but we know that a student needs our honesty so she can sift through her repertory of interests and personal strengths and begin to find the connections that are the most powerful for her. By guiding girls to be more self-aware, we inspire and encourage them to make those associations, to be in their element. This work happens every time we say to a student, "See what you achieved! What made that possible? How did you manage to move that project along? Find that solution? Decide on that course of action?" By asking girls to reflect and take stock of their unique contributions, we give them permission to imagine abundant venues for their passion and talent in the many years to come.

Tips & Tactics

Make it routine to ask your daughter how she has contributed to positive outcomes. Girls easily dismiss their unique attributes and the ways those attributes affect change. Hidden among her personal characteristics, however, are some of the essential modules your daughter will use to construct a purposeful life. The more aware she is of her strengths, the more informed her decisions will be about future pursuits.

65. The Confidence to Be
Growing into Uniqueness

There was a small workroom at the back of my fifth-grade classroom at Emerson Elementary School, and that's where I was allowed to go to draw when I finished my assignments early. Actually, it wasn't drawing; it was tracing flowers. Mrs. Stevens, my teacher, had a box of heavy white cards with detailed, black-outlined drawings of irises, jonquils, and hyacinths. I would lay a piece of tracing paper over the drawing, follow the outline with my pen, and color it in. Mrs. Stevens would then decorate the blank walls above the chalkboard with my art. In hindsight, inviting me to read a book or handing me a sheet of fractions to add might have done me more good. However, the reward of being allowed to leave the classroom and color set me apart and confirmed my feeling of being distinct and unique.

It is during the teen years that girls begin to set themselves apart in earnest. Prospective Miss Hall's School students frequently tell us during their admission interviews that they need a new school with new opportunities. One girl said a few years ago, "I was following along in my old school until one day I said, 'I want so much more for myself.' So, I stepped out of line and came here." This girl was searching for the place where she could discover more about who she was and where she could catch a glimpse of her unique, authentic self, the source of her greatness.

Becoming one's own person is the vital work that begins in the teen years. It happens best, we believe, in an environment that confirms, validates, and gives reliable responses to girls and asks them to reflect on their experiences. It also happens best in a setting where adults believe that a girl's individuality has layers of complexity and can't be boiled down to grades alone. Our goal at Miss Hall's School is for each girl to come to know herself well. As she gains new insight into herself, she has only to look around to find myriad opportunities for taking her emerging adult self out for a test drive.

Experiences that allow student interaction with the world at large on a regular, structured basis, such as those offered through the school's community-service, experiential-learning program, provide a curriculum for self-awareness by expanding the points of connection for girls. Just as a girl is learning more about herself, she is observing and interacting with the larger world in her on-site work. In this real-world laboratory, she begins to make connections between her unique set of skills and attributes and the tasks, situations, challenges, and opportunities that surround her. Most importantly, as she engages with her work, she receives confirmation, correction, and validation. She wants to discover more about what she can do. Her competency deepens, and although there are setbacks, she learns that she can have confidence in her opinions, ability, and judgment.

In a *Newsweek* interview about her book *Confidence: How Winning Streaks and Losing Streaks Begin and End*, Rosabeth Moss Kanter, who specializes in and writes frequently about innovation and leadership for change, defines confidence as "the expectation of a positive outcome."[298] That confidence is rooted in self-knowledge. Another dimension of this subject was defined by Carl Jung, who wrote, "In knowing ourselves to be unique in our personal combination . . . we possess also the capacity for becoming conscious of the infinite. But only then!"[299] By understanding and embracing their uniqueness, adolescent girls deepen and broaden their understanding of their purpose in the world.

Kanter has also said, "If you hold back, you don't try, and you don't know how good your ideas are."[300] When girls expect positive results and use the talents that are uniquely theirs to influence outcomes and to effect change, they come to know just how good their ideas are.

Tips & Tactics

The next time your daughter has time on her hands, ask her to write a recommendation for herself. She could imagine she is her college counselor or English teacher writing to colleges on her behalf, or she could imagine she is her personal reference writing to support her candidacy for a job. Girls sometimes struggle to name their personal skills and attributes. If this task is daunting for your daughter, have a conversation with her about what you see as her personal strengths, and then ask her to try again.

A word of caution: girls often limit their cataloguing of strengths to those that have to do with taking care of others. If that is the case with your daughter, guide her to go beyond those skills to others that pertain to her intellectual, athletic, artistic, decision-making, and problem-solving competencies.

66. Better to Forgive
Taking Advantage of Second Chances

I don't remember dumping a glass of Welch's grape juice on the gray wool fabric, but I've heard the story many times. My mother had been preoccupied for five months with horrific morning sickness made only worse by the heat and humidity of a Midwest summer. A great aunt, who doted on me and who had come to help out, had returned home. And I, at four years old, was fairly certain that I needed more attention. So one September afternoon as my mother sat sewing a gray flannel jacket, I gave her a long, defiant look and slowly but very surely tipped over a large glass of sticky, purple liquid, soaking as much of the garment as possible.

Although my memory doesn't reach back far enough to let me recall this event, the fact that my mother still reminds me of it so many years later suggests that I did, in fact, get her attention. Fortunately for me, I wasn't banished from the house for my misstep. My parents understood, forgave me, and gave me a second chance, the first of many.

Forgiveness has a place in our work with adolescent girls here at Miss Hall's School. How educators respond to the missteps of students reflects in part the central ethos of the institution. Our response also communicates our understanding of adolescent development.

We are in the business, after all, of educating girls. In class, when a girl makes a mistake or does poorly on a quiz or test, we devoutly hope that she can do better next time. We use the weak moments as indicators of what a girl does not yet know but can learn. So it is with discipline. A girl may have difficulty in understanding or accepting the rationale behind school rules. She may be confused, or she may be reacting to any of a variety of factors. Whatever the reason, we have the opportunity to help her learn more about herself and about the requirements of the world. We have the opportunity to help her grow and improve.

When girls make mistakes, the school provides the intervention and consequences but also the conditions for redemption. We offer the response that we would want for ourselves: firm admonishment, clear explanation, an assurance of continued respect and support, and an implicit understanding that we are all in this together. Even in cases when it is in everyone's best interest for a student to leave the school, we always hope that the separation is for her, in the long run, a positive, transforming experience.

When I meet with a girl who has had difficulty, I tell her that she is lucky. She has been able to see a weakness in herself and has been given the opportunity to deal with it. If we had not intervened, if no sanction had occurred, that weak spot would still be there, hidden and offering no possibility for change. As teachers, we try to bring to our students an understanding of the universality of what adolescent girls are going through and of our obligation to create the conditions for their learning.

Another aspect of creating the conditions for forgiveness in the school community is that we want to model forgiveness for students. Adolescents struggle with letting go of anger and disappointment. They can get tangled up in the distinction between forgiving someone for a wrong and condoning the wrong. For girls' own well being, we want them to learn, as author and authority on forgiveness therapy Frederic Luskin explains, that forgiveness is "taking back your power . . . taking responsibility for how you feel . . . [and] being the hero instead of the victim."[301] These are the lessons we strive always to teach because girls must learn them in order to have lives of their own making.

I am grateful that my mother forgave me. In thinking about that jacket, I don't remember hearing what happened to it. Purple juice on gray wool sounds serious. Maybe I should offer to replace it.

Tips & Tactics

Think twice before you rush in to eliminate the opportunity for your daughter to apologize for her misstep. It is through taking responsibility for her shortfalls that she has the chance to understand more about herself and to learn from you how to forgive. Knowing how being forgiven feels, she is better able to give that gift to others.

67. How Can I Help?
Making a Difference

I don't remember anyone talking about volunteerism when I was growing up. In my hometown people just came to the rescue anytime there was a need. My family (and all the families I knew) took care not only of each other but also of those in the community who needed help, whether or not we knew them by name. Providing food, clothing, or rides to the doctor was just something one did because it needed doing.

Not unlike values that once were modeled and thus taught informally in closely connected communities, volunteering is now frequently vested in formal programs. At Miss Hall's School, we include service learning in our curriculum because its concepts are linked to responsible citizenship and because serving others is good for the developing adolescent psyche. It is beneficial for teenagers to be reminded that, in the words of Winston Churchill, "we make a living by what we get, but we make a life by what we give."[302] Cultivating the habit of volunteering on behalf of those in need is an important goal of the program.

This is not to suggest that adolescents wouldn't be inclined to help others if the program didn't exist. According to the faculty advisor to the school's student council, "The minute girls hear that someone needs something, they want to help. The difficulty comes in trying to narrow their focus to match the energy and dollars available." Students have rallied behind many local, national, and international initiatives to aid those in need. Some of the projects were designed by groups of girls. Others, however, were the ideas of single students who wanted to do something to make a difference.

As Americans ushered in the twenty-first century, there was much discussion about the state of civil society in the United States and about whether as a country we were steadily disengaging from each other and our communities. However, in the face of recent disasters, both in the United States and elsewhere in the world, there is evidence in daily news reports that our willingness to reach out and get involved doesn't appear to be as feeble as some might have thought. Whether this evidence signals a resurgence in civic and political engagement remains to be seen. What interests those of us who parent and teach girls is the long and richly deep legacy of women coming together to effect change.

Although at the time that Mira Hall established her school women could not vote, they were organizing effectively to address social problems created, in part, by growing industrialization and urbanization. Jane Addams and Vida Scudder (a classmate of Miss Hall's at Smith College in the mid-1880s) represent a large group of women reformers who set up settlements to provide such services as day care and health care for the poor working class in large cities. Women coming together in volunteer organizations fueled much of the reform of what we now call the Progressive Era.

We want girls to value this legacy and incorporate civic responsibility into their emerging young-woman vision. Using Tracy Gary and Melissa Kohner's *Inspired Philanthropy: Creating a Giving Plan: A Workbook*, the school's student council has created its own philanthropic mission statement as an approach to managing its philanthropic initiatives. The issue for girls is not whether they will reach out to others, but rather how they will make informed decisions in light of limited resources. "Creating a giving plan has been a tool not just to help organize my mail," writes Gary, "but to bring to light what my own consciousness and intuition would have me prioritize given the needs around me."[303] This is a powerful and transformative process for girls to undertake because, as Gary puts it, the approach allows individuals "to be in better balance between reflection, vision and their actions."[304]

The world is waiting for our young women and the actions they will take throughout their lives. As teachers and parents, we must take the time now to listen to adolescent girls talk about their passions, those issues about which they care deeply. In this way, we encourage each girl to connect her vision of how to make the world a better place with her bedrock belief in her ability to accomplish the task.

Tips & Tactics

It is good practice for your daughter to learn how to develop a focus for the volunteering or fundraising she wants to undertake. Once a year (perhaps on her birthday), suggest that she think about causes that are most important to her and that she write down what she would like to support and why. Teaching her to examine her reasons for reaching out to others helps her learn about her values.

68. Great Expectations
Teaching Excellence

I could not believe my good luck when I was assigned to Mr. Humble. He was the most distinguished and respected piano professor at my college, and he would be my teacher. Everyone knew that if you had Mr. Humble, a gentle, soft-spoken man somewhere in his late sixties, you were among a chosen few. He was the best, his standards were high, and he expected his students to work hard.

It is the teachers who expected only our best and who inspired us to work hard whom we remember. When alumnae recall faculty members who had the most impact on their lives, they inevitably describe those teachers who required the most from them. Adolescents may resist and complain about demanding work, but it is their victory over the struggle and their accomplishment in producing work of quality that have enduring value.

In their eloquent and inspiring book *The Elements of Teaching*, James M. Banner Jr. and Harold C. Cannon describe the requirements of ethical teaching and include in the list the requirement of setting high standards and expectations and inspiring students to meet them.[305] As an example of how one teacher inspires her students, the authors share a motto she writes on the board each day: "Choose a high failure rather than a low success."[306] In other words, ethical teaching requires us, as Banner and Cannon write, to "inspire [our] students to stretch and thus to grow in knowledge and understanding."[307]

A controversy about education being played out in the news media might seem to pit high standards and expectations against creative, student-centered teaching. But this argument creates a false dichotomy. Maintaining high standards does not squeeze the intellectual life out of classrooms or pull teachers off the real business of teaching. Content and facts are not at cross purposes with intellectual pursuit. The virtue of rigor is that it pulls teenagers out of themselves. By requiring adolescent girls to learn the specifics of zygote formation as well as to understand what the framers of the First Amendment meant by "an establishment of religion," we prevent girls from staying locked inside small thoughts. Insisting that our students grapple with difficult stuff allows us to lead them beyond the presumption and self-indulgence that define the adolescent years.

Our job as teachers and as parents is to help adolescent girls expand their knowledge, to insist they learn as much as possible so they have a greater understanding of themselves and the world around them. We cannot allow girls to ignore their own untapped potential. Through challenging, thoughtful study, girls begin to clarify their thinking about who they are and what they are capable of accomplishing. Girls' deepest, truest, and most original thinking will grow out of their struggles to understand the provocative thoughts of those who have gone before them.

How tempting it is to lower the bar when the going gets rough! But we know that when we do, we are nothing more than accomplices to the self-doubt that robs an adolescent girl of her potential. We expect adolescents to become weary and to resist. Nevertheless, it is the duty of teachers, as Banner and Cannon say, to "lead their students to set their own high expectations, to imagine what they may achieve, and to aspire to achieve it."[308] When we do that, we pay the highest level of respect to young women.

This is exactly what Mr. Humble did. I simply would not disappoint him or myself. And when I played very well, he quietly said, "Good." That meant the world to me. From this exceptional teacher, I learned two life lessons: scholarship demanded my best effort, and I was worthy of respect.

Passion for the challenge of rigorous work and respect for the individual are the gifts we give our students when we are doing our best work.

Tips & Tactics

It is tempting when a daughter is overwhelmed with challenging work for parents to give her a pass or offer an escape route. When we give in to that temptation, we run the risk of communicating to her that we don't believe she is up to the challenge. Enable your daughter's strength by acknowledging her feelings ("I can tell what a difficult assignment this is") and then confirm her strength to tackle the project ("What strategies have you used before to work through a project like this? Might they work now? Whom might you find to coach you in getting started?").

69. Oops, Sorry
Connecting through Conversational Tics

I t went like this:

Example 1:
My dad: "I just heard that George got a new job."
My mom: "Did George get a new job?"
My dad: "That's what I just said."

Example 2:
My dad (after arriving home from a church board meeting): "I guess we'll be repaving the church parking lot."
My mom: "I didn't know that."
My dad: "Mildred, you couldn't have known it. We just decided tonight."

My mother's comments are examples of the conversational tics, seemingly useless phrases, that I was accustomed to hearing in everyday banter in my hometown. My dad, who took them literally, is the only one I can remember who challenged them. Usually, such expressions were slid into casual chitchat with nary a notice. From time to time, I hear myself, even now, dropping them into conversations. Although they may appear to be nonsensical and add little in the way of content to a discussion, they typically sustain engagement and signal that one is listening and wishes to continue talking.

Recently, a teacher and coach here at Miss Hall's School told me about another type of verbal tic, the *empty sorry*, that she had been hearing on the volleyball court. She had noticed that during practice when girls missed serves or failed to return the ball, they frequently chirped, "Sorry." The coach decided to ask the team members what they were apologizing for. When the girls had time to reflect, they realized that the apology had become a distracting substitute for what they actually wanted to do. With their coach's guidance, the team agreed that a more appropriate response when serves go awry would be to maintain focus and later seek extra coaching.

Not long after I learned about the empty sorry discussion, I saw several articles reporting on recent research that found that women apologize more than men. It is not that women have more to apologize for than men do, the research found.[309] It is, rather, that women have "a lower threshold [than men] for what is offensive behavior."[310] Compared with men, women simply identify more instances where they believe an apology is needed. The lead researcher in the study speculated that this apology habit may also be related to women being "more concerned with the emotional experiences of others and in promoting harmony in their relationships."[311] In other words, women see more possibilities of relationships going off track and thus act accordingly to maintain them.

Girls, too, are very invested in sustaining the important relationships in their lives, and we must remember this as we teach and guide them. It would be easy, for example, to jump to the conclusion that the mea culpa habit reflects low self-esteem in a daughter. Author and professor of linguistics Deborah Tannen debunks that diagnosis and explains that there can be far more involved in the issue than we might think.[312] In fact, she says that apologetic vocabulary is "one of many conversational rituals by which women take the other person's experience into account."[313]

The apologies on the volleyball court were, perhaps, athletes taking the impatience of the receivers into account when the ball failed to go over the net and saying, in effect, "I'm sorry to waste your time." In a different setting, I can hear a girl saying, "I'm sorry," when her friend tells her that she and her boyfriend have broken up. The expression communicates empathy and understanding of what her friend is experiencing. Tannen explains that "I'm sorry," in this situation, may be more a way of saying, "I'm sorry that happened."[314] In other words, "This use of *sorry* is focused outward, taking into account the experience of the person you're talking to."[315] Ascribing self-confidence problems to the behavior, therefore, "misinterprets this other-focused strategy as if it revealed the speaker's inner state."[316]

As I round corners here at Miss Hall's School, I often hear girls say, "Oops, sorry," as we near a collision. I find that instinctively I do the same. Tannen calls this type of quick apology an "automatic courtesy, like a verbal tipping of the hat."[317] Again, this is not about anyone being at fault. Rather, it is another example of outward focus: a girl's "Oops, sorry" is her giving notice that she knows there has been a bobble.[318]

In teaching and parenting girls, we acknowledge and validate their instincts and understand the healthy rituals, in this case conversational, that they use to strengthen their connectedness with others. Sometimes we step in, as the volleyball coach did, and ask girls to reflect on what they're saying. Then when those times come along that require not a conversational "Sorry" but a full and heartfelt apology, we stand by girls and confirm their courage to be sincere and honorable.

Tips & Tactics

Take note of your daughter's conversational tics. In what ways does she acknowledge others' feelings? Interject a comment to promote harmony in a relationship? Signal to someone that she understands their situation? Talk with your daughter about how she uses language in everyday conversations so that she is aware of what she is doing and can assess for herself whether she is being true to herself in what she says.

70. Staying Connected
Relationships and Life

Snapshots from the school: a cluster of girls in front of the weekend activities bulletin board deciding where to spend Saturday afternoon; girls rushing to greet multiple best friends back from vacation; girls cheering for a fellow student's birthday; sixteen girls having an impromptu meeting in a dorm room built for two. A girl can be off by herself, safely supported from afar, but that is not the rule. The rule is connection. Miss Hall's School is home to ever-shifting, forming and re-forming, excited, hushed, intense, laughing clumps of adolescent girls.

There is growing research to support the hypothesis that being connected keeps us healthy and, in fact, extends life. In his book *Connect: 12 Vital Ties That Open Your Heart, Lengthen Your Life, and Deepen Your Soul*, psychiatrist Edward M. Hallowell says that along with our daily vitamin C tablet, we need a daily "dose of the human moment—positive contact with other people."[319] Furthermore, studies have confirmed, according to Hallowell, that students who feel a connectedness in two domains—family and school—have high grades and self-esteem and are least likely to use illegal substances.[320]

Whatever is true about the benefits of connectedness for adolescents in general is more so for adolescent girls. One does not have to spend much time around girls to know that life for them is *all* about connections. So is school. Ask any girl how school is going, and she'll tell you about her relationships with teachers and friends. School is good if a girl's connections to faculty and peers are good. Otherwise, school is a drudge. In Karen Stabiner's book *All Girls: Single-Sex Education and Why it Matters*, psychologist and researcher JoAnn Deak is quoted as saying that a teacher "who can grab the heart and head of a girl will do better than a teacher who only grabs her head."[321]

One of the great strengths of any school is the presence of teachers who understand this. Many of us adults can recall teachers who made such indelible connections that we remember them vividly after twenty, thirty, or even forty years. The small size of a school can be a major factor in establishing ties. At Miss Hall's School, faculty members fill many roles, and students have teachers who are also their advisors, hall moms, and coaches. In any school setting, however, the essential connections required for learning will be formed when a girl is surrounded by teachers who know her well, are committed to her growth, and make it their job to grab her heart.

Connectedness is far more than meaningful relationships, however. As Deak reminds us in *How Girls Thrive: An Essential Guide for Educators (and Parents)*, connectedness is a girl's lens for moral orientation.[322] Nearly thirty years ago, adolescent-development researcher Carol Gilligan first pointed out in her book *In a Different Voice: Psychological Theory and Women's Development* that connectedness is at the center of moral decision making for females. For women and girls, "morality lies in recognizing connection."[323] As a result, girls dealing with moral dilemmas often find themselves wondering whether, as Gilligan says, "to keep friendship or keep justice."[324] Although an adolescent girl knows that cheating is wrong, when the decision is whether or not to let a friend copy from her test paper, the conflict is between doing what's right and supporting a friend. Understanding this, we work with girls to help them find ways to maintain relationships while upholding their own values.

I often cite Deak's three Cs, her critical components of self-esteem: competence, confidence, and connectedness.[325] She says that it is clear that focusing on oneself alone only increases selfishness.[326] When an adolescent girl can focus outward and connect with other human beings, her interests are broadened. She begins to accept the idea that life is not all about her but about the contributions she will make.

A special challenge for teachers and parents is being able to redefine connectedness as girls get older. It is comforting to know that we don't have to let go of the connections we have so painstakingly developed and value so much. We do have to realize, however, that girls need different kinds of support as they move from dependent ninth graders to the self-reliance of early adulthood. The reward is in the deep satisfaction we feel, as parents and teachers, when we are able to sustain healthy relationships through growth and change.

Tips & Tactics

From time to time, it is beneficial to reflect on the basis of the connection we have with our daughters. The goal is not to sustain connections by becoming a concierge service, indulging a daughter's every whim. Nor can we believe that the only way to stay connected is to become our daughter's friend, overlooking her missteps and giving her carte blanche to do as she pleases. The goal is to sustain our connection by fostering her growth toward becoming a self-reliant young adult.

71. Facing Up to Facebook
Friendship and Community in a Virtual World

Nancy and I were best friends, inseparable from the ages of five through eleven. We knew each other well, shared hours of fun, and stuck it out through setbacks. (She dropped my china tea set and backed out of going with me on a family vacation. I would hate to see her list for me!) By high school, Nancy and I had outgrown each other, and my community of friends had expanded. Now we were a little band of girls, agonizing over homework, fretting about acne, meeting at the Dairy Queen, singing "Roses are Red," dancing the twist, and stitching together the pages of our high-school years.

The notions of friendship and community have changed since the sixties, and the girls now attending Miss Hall's School have experienced both very differently than those of us not born in a virtual age. In a recent article, literary critic and author William Deresiewicz offers an overview of how friendship has evolved over the centuries and describes how we have moved from a classical idea of "one true friend," or friendships that are "precious" and "hard-won," to "faux friendships" that are served up on Internet sites like Facebook.[327] According to Deresiewicz, we are seduced by our virtual connections into thinking that we have lots of friends and that we are part of a community.[328] Instead, we have only "a 'sense' of community . . . the feeling without the structure; a private emotion, not a collective experience."[329]

In order to become self-aware and to be prepared for full and purposeful lives, our daughters must have an abundance of collective experiences, in real time and with real people. It is in living with others, day in and day out and over time, that girls learn about themselves and about how to manage their own needs in relation to those who are doing the same. One of the reasons a boarding-school community like that of Miss Hall's School is such a transformational setting is that girls can work collectively with each other and their teachers to learn and practice the skills they need to develop.

Most of these skills involve interacting face-to-face with other individuals. Deresiewicz points out, however, that the virtual world into which these girls were born encourages them to stop thinking of others as individuals.[330] It is far more common for teens in today's culture to post personal status reports and updates to five hundred friends on Facebook than to share their thoughts with others face-to-face. We have turned friends into an "indiscriminate mass . . . a faceless public," Deresiewicz says.[331] Needless to say, Miss Hall's School students do use Facebook, and girls also routinely use the school's e-mail to send messages to the whole community ("Help! I've lost my keys!"). When a student is worried that her solid B in her calculus course is sliding into the C range, however, she learns to solve her problem by walking down the hall, sitting down with her teacher, and working one-on-one until she understands what she will need to do to get back on track.

Resolving interpersonal squabbles must also be done in person. Is it any wonder in a virtual age, when the audience is faceless, that we read about teens feeling empowered to vent their frustrations electronically? It takes no bravery or finesse to post offensive, harassing, and threatening messages when you are in, to use Deresiewicz's term, "an electronic cave."[332]

Working through disagreements and conflicts personally, however, requires courage and skill, and the boarding environment provides ample opportunities to become competent in these areas. Recently, the school's seniors were reviewing techniques for successful conflict resolution. The head resident reminded me that the girls began learning these skills in the ninth grade. "We recall the behaviors they used when they were younger," she said, "and they remember how ineffective nonverbal communication, like the eye roll or pretending not to see your roommate, was." Now, as young women a few months from moving on to college, these students have a toolbox of skills to use in settling disputes, skills that require direct and respectful communication in real time with real individuals.

Perhaps the most powerful experiences we can provide in this actual community are those that have to do with girls learning to take healthy risks, to be comfortable with mistakes, and to recover and move on. The girl who goes to see her teacher because she sees her grade dropping learns that she is not alone in stumbling in that portion of the test and is asked to be the teacher the next day, now that she has become the expert. A girl who misses her foul shot learns that when she redoubles her effort, she gets her rebound and scores two points. The girl who misjudges the time it takes to complete her research project learns that time-management tips provide what she needs to turn in her assignment earlier next time around. In strong communities where people know and are committed to each other, it is safe to take a risk, safe to fail, and possible to recover.

We want our daughters to continue to develop self-awareness at all stages of their lives. Teaching girls in their teen years how to be true to themselves while forging meaningful relationships based on mutual growth and understanding will give them the skills they need to sustain precious and hard-won partnerships throughout their lives.

Tips & Tactics

Take stock of how much of your daughter's day is spent in developing relationships with real people in real time. Does her school environment offer her a community of peers and adults with whom she can engage in meaningful ways? Have you and your daughter agreed on how she will conduct herself on social-networking sites? Is your daughter developing the interpersonal skills she needs to relate to others in person and with confidence and respect? If you are worried that she is losing touch with the real world, it is your job as a parent to help her reconnect.

72. A Community Together
Growing Up amid Cultural Isolation

When I walked among the school library's bookshelves some time ago, a book title caught my eye: *A Tribe Apart: A Journey into the Heart of American Adolescence* by Patricia Hersch. My first thought went back to a conversation I had recently with a senior staff member about how out of touch we are with some aspects of current teenage culture. Case in point: I heard a few students talking recently about a Lady Gaga concert coming up in the fall in a nearby city. Lady who? I feel a tribe apart when I don't even have name recognition.

However, Hersch's book is a serious comment on the gulf that exists between today's teens and the adult community. Whereas adolescents have always wanted to hang out together, teenagers in our current society are left on their own, says Hersch.[333] "In the vacuum where traditional behavioral expectations for young people used to exist, in the silence of empty homes and neighborhoods," Hersch writes, "young people have built their own community."[334]

We are all familiar with cultural changes that have isolated families and contributed to a loose connection between adults and teens. Grandparents, aunts, and uncles no longer live down the street, sprawling suburbs have taken the place of tight-knit neighborhoods, concern for safety keeps kids inside and discourages friendly interaction with local townspeople, and working parents means children spend hours alone before Mom and Dad return in the evening. What interested me about Hersch's perspective, however, were the observations she makes regarding how those of us who were teenagers in the sixties have approached our own parenting.

We were, as she says, the in-your-face generation. Large and powerful, the baby-boomer cohort muscled its way into a contentious relationship with parents. Those who count themselves part of this postwar demographic bulge know that they were against almost everything their parents were for. Teenagers in the sixties were perceived, as Hersch says, as a "defiant horde . . . an army of youth," and thus the ""tribal notion was here to stay."[335]

Even those of us who were slightly out of the main frame of this rebellious time (in Joplin, Missouri, we lingered in the fifties long after the decade had passed) agree with Hersch that during the sixties everything was open to debate. We were a generation demanding freedom and space and refusing to accept the established ways of behaving. As a result, we understand our own children's needs to be free of our control because that's what we demanded when we were their age. But we're not any more comfortable than our parents were about imposing no restrictions. How much space do kids need? How much should adults intrude? As Hersch says, "Parents who grew up in the sixties find such issues confusing."[336] My conversations with today's parents indicate that the baby boomers have no monopoly on confusion when it comes to setting boundaries for offspring.

It is interesting to consider this situation in the context of a society that has changed dramatically in the last half century. When our parents were unsure of how to handle elbowing adolescents, they had an entire community to call on. It's not as easy for today's parents, with no extended family close by, to get a quick tip from a wise elder or an experienced neighbor. When I disagreed with my parents and went elsewhere for advice, I heard the same basic message. Today we live in communities where most often there is not a broadly shared consensus about what is right or wrong. Frequently, we don't agree with the way the parents of our daughters' friends make decisions. Many times I heard my daughters say, "I'm the only one who's not being allowed to . . ."

There is also the simple issue of time and energy. Both are in shorter supply today than when I grew up. Hersch sums up the dilemma modern-day parents of teens face: "Everything is open to debate and unfortunately there isn't time, consensus, or perhaps will to figure it out. So the issues are thrown back on the kids."[337]

Thinking about all this made me want to hear a current student's reaction to some of these ideas. I sat down to talk with a new boarding student, a girl who had attended a large public high school and who came to Miss Hall's School as a junior. "What do you think about this tribe apart business?" I asked her. "How tightly connected is the teenage community? Are we, as adults, out of touch?"

Her comments were fascinating. As we would expect, the ties of teen friendship are strong. "My friends are so important," she explained, and, yes, the notion of the teenage culture being distinct and separate—a tribe apart—resonated strongly with her. But we moved beyond that expected answer to a deeper insight, poignantly expressed. "It's so hard getting through these years," she said. She went on to describe all the competing desires—fitting in, being accepted, maintaining friendships, making good grades, playing well in her chosen sport, and in general, meeting not only her parents' expectations but her own as well. How to keep everything together and walk that delicate line without stumbling or falling was foremost in this girl's mind. Her comments indicated that her need to be supported by a community was far greater than her need to be isolated from adults.

The interesting thing about this story is how the boarding-school experience fits in. While it provides a community for adolescents, it also is related daily to the adult world. Girls, therefore, have the opportunity to develop their independence and to do that within the continuity of a healthy adult culture. Here in this place where we know teenagers well and maintain connections with them and their families, girls are parts of the whole.

Tips & Tactics

Your daughter needs to be with friends and also to have the space to develop into her own person. Furthermore, she needs to know that there are boundaries and that you are involved in setting those boundaries. In the best of all worlds, parents work together in defining limits. If that is not possible, find other adults in whom you can confide. Parenting is easier when we feel part of a community of support.

73. Making Cool Decisions
Minimizing Unhealthy Risks

"Cool down!" is what Dad would say when I got heated up over how short I could wear my skirt, how late I could stay up, or when I could next have the car. Sometimes when I really didn't like the answer, I would find myself slamming doors and screaming at my parents. I didn't plan to be out of control, but in the heat of the moment, that's what happened. Then I had to deal with the consequences: a time-out in my room or a forfeited night out with friends.

In the *New York Times Magazine* article "The Futile Pursuit of Happiness," researchers discuss what they call the "empathy gap."[338] This is our inability to predict how we will behave in a hot, or agitated, state when we are in a cold, or calm, state. Happiness is affected, as one psychologist says, because "if our decision making is influenced by these transient emotional and psychological states, then we know we're not making decisions with an eye toward future consequences."[339]

As adults, we have no problem understanding the empathy gap. How many times have we been swept into a decision by the circumstances of the moment and regretted it later? Did you ever go over your limit at an auction? Invite thirty people to dinner? Convince yourself that not only do you need the newest technological gadget but you need the high-end version with all the bells and whistles? If we can override good judgment in the heat of the moment, imagine how much more vulnerable our daughters are! No wonder we worry!

There is strong evidence of the likelihood that teens will make impulsive decisions because of what we now know about how adolescent brains develop. Neurologist Francis Jensen says that teens think differently than adults because the frontal lobes "are not fully connected."[340] As she explains, "It's the part of the brain that says: 'Is this a good idea? What is the consequence of this action?'"[341] It isn't until the mid-twenties, in fact, that the myelin, the fatty coating that facilitates efficient neural communication, is sufficiently developed to allow young people to be more adept at anticipating outcomes of their actions.[342] (Keep that in mind the next time your teenager says she wants to go skydiving!)

We know that adolescent girls make lots of sense when they are in focused conversations about the perils of risky behavior. They can talk the talk about the hazards of smoking, the risks of unprotected sex, or the danger of riding with someone who has been drinking. As Jensen points out, "It's not that [teens] don't have a frontal lobe. . . . But they're going to access it more slowly."[343] With this insight, we can understand that in the rush of a moment when danger is present, a teen can find herself taking a risk because the neurons that allow her to think a situation through and anticipate consequences are just not firing fast enough.

What can we do to minimize the chances that girls will make unwise decisions? One of the most powerful factors in the healthy development of teens is the influence of a strong community that surrounds a girl with clear, consistent, and affirming messages. At Miss Hall's School, an environment with round-the-clock values, adults are ready and willing to talk with girls whenever they need help in untangling the knotted threads of adolescence. The messages that are communicated about those values help a girl create inner boundaries that will provide the context for her thinking when she must make quick choices about what to do next.

Positive peer pressure is another essential stabilizing factor for girls. It is often the case that teens cannot heed advice until it is delivered by a friend their own age. With that in mind, I remind the school's senior class at the beginning of every academic year that they will be watched by younger girls and often will be seen as role models. Therefore, I expect them to honor the trust we have placed in them.

Since risk taking is the domain of the teenager, our job as parents and as teachers is also to offer a buffet of healthy risks. Encouraging a girl to try out for the musical, to learn to play soccer, to offer an opposing argument in a classroom discussion, or to bring her suggestions for recycling to the head of school will help to curb the adolescent appetite for unhealthy risk taking and allow a girl to discover new talent and strengths in the process.

Knowing that the time will come when an adolescent girl's frontal lobes will be working more efficiently, we concentrate in the high-school years on helping her acquire a database of values and information that will have more meaning to her down the road. In other words, we believe that what she learns now will stand her in good stead for that point in her twenties when the myelin is fully developed, her mind clears, and she is a new adult, prepared to make considered choices and decisions.

Tips & Tactics

When your daughter missteps, find time to talk with her about what she should have done versus what she did. Having her reflect on what prevented her from doing what *she knew was right* is the first step in raising her awareness about where she may be most vulnerable to peer pressure.

•••

Ask your teen to make a list of values or ideals that mean the most to her. (She may need you to give her examples, such as honesty or respect.) Then ask her to explain why these particular values were chosen. Suggest that she keep the list handy and consult it to see what guidance it can provide the next time she is struggling with relationships or with a decision.

74. The More the Merrier
Collaboration and Creativity

Our shows were produced in our family dining room, where my piano stood and where the table could be slid aside to give us more floor space. Best friend Nancy and I were the producers. My little brother and other younger kids from the block joined in to think up acts, make up jokes, design the costumes, and create the flyers to hand to neighbors. With planning complete and using a dressing screen (which I had seen Ginger Rogers and Betty Grable use in old movies), we changed into various garbs, then stepped out onto the "stage" to sing, dance, and perform our skits. Recently I called my brother to see what he remembered about our shows, and his memory was of wearing tights and a cape. "Who were you?" I asked, reminded of the costume but not the role. "The Lone Ranger," he answered. But of course.

I don't remember details about the songs or skits, but I do remember the experience of pooling ideas on those Saturday mornings so long ago. "How 'bout this?" someone would say, and someone else would jump in with, "No, let's do this!" It was collaboration that spurred the creativity.

In an essay about economic power in the twenty-first century, *New York Times* columnist David Brooks notes what we already know, that innovation and creativity fuel economic growth in the current information age. He predicts that the nation that will define the new epoch, therefore, will be the one with the "thickest and most expansive networks" for sharing ideas.[344] He includes in his essay Harvard psychologist Howard Gardner's description of a creative person: "She . . . finds a group of people who share her passions and interests . . . [and] gets involved with a team to create something amazing."[345]

At a recent morning meeting here at Miss Hall's School, girls from our community-service club presented the creative work they had been doing. Several club members talked about their fundraising projects and about the organizations they were supporting. One of these was another student group, a new initiative that uses microlending to help women in developing countries around the world start businesses. A student club that supports another student club that supports women half a world away is a productive network, I thought.

With Brooks's comment about the collaborative nature of creativity and the girls' presentation fresh in mind, I met with a few students to hear what they thought about creative collaboration. "Ideas just flow when girls come together," said one student. Referencing what happens in theatrical productions, another girl mentioned that if everyone isn't "emotionally alive *together*, the performance is a flop." I liked the imagery in this comment from a student who noted that, with many participating, ideas "bubble up and spread out, and people are inspired." Two students referenced academic collaboration. In math class, each girl contributes one solution to a problem, and collaboratively the class pools those ideas to arrive at the best approach. "In English class," a second girl explained, "we don't see the relevance of the passage until someone says something, the discussion begins, and, suddenly, we all see the relevance!"

As educators, we believe collaboration is creative when individuals bring to it a depth of self-knowledge and considerable inner resources. Indeed, much of our work is focused on helping each girl develop confidence in her inner self. This means not only having an idea of one's own but also having the skill to resolve conflict without resort to passive-aggressive strategies.

With that piece in place, our students' appreciation for collaborative work and their quick and insightful descriptions of the value they place on it reflect an important part of what they are learning. Just as we help a girl to understand parabolic motion and how to conjugate irregular French verbs, we are also teaching her the skills she needs to engage in respectful debate and manage conflict directly. Thus when a girl says, as one did in our discussion, that projects get done "when we all work with shared interest and passion toward a single purpose," I believe that she is on the road to discovering how to partner with others toward the greater goal of having influence in the world.

Tips & Tactics

Ask your daughter if she engages with others in projects at school. Are they experiences she enjoys? If so, ask her to tell you why. If she says that she does not enjoy collaborative assignments, ask her if she can tell you why that is. Listen for indications that your daughter perceives difficulty with the students she is asked to partner with on projects. (Perhaps she believes others don't do their share of the work. Or perhaps she senses that others in the group don't like her.) Ask her if she has been able to talk openly about these worries. Our young women will be expected to work effectively with others in future pursuits. Resolving difficulties and being able to advocate for one's needs are skills girls need to learn and practice.

75. Life's Syntax
Teaching Fluency in Knowledge

With a new driver's license and keys in hand, I hopped into the car, my destination the McCunes. They were our closest friends while I was growing up, more like an aunt and uncle to me. I was first at their house as an infant, and by the time I was pulling out of our driveway to make my first solo trip at sixteen, I had probably been driven there with my folks every week of every year I'd been alive. In other words, a lot. What I remember about this time, however, is getting to the corner, making the turn onto 20th Street, and then having absolutely no idea what to do next. Back I went to get directions. My parents were incredulous. "What do you mean, you don't know how to get there?" they asked in stunned disbelief. I doubt that I had an answer for them then, but it's clear now. I didn't know because I had no need to know before the moment I sat behind the wheel.

Point-of-need instructions, directions on how to do something at the moment one needs to know, are all around us. We're all familiar with the sign near the parking garage elevator (Level 2—Green Level) or the sign on the copy machine (Help). Some Mexican restaurants print drawings on napkins to guide the diner in folding a burrito. Navigating the computer is all about clicking for information at the moment that it's useful. Learning this way makes sense, and we certainly use the point-of-need approach in teaching girls at Miss Hall's School.

If we want adolescents truly to be successful as adults, however, we must go beyond the click-here strategies to the level of teaching that molds girls' minds as learners and embeds in them the structures that will allow them to make sense of the world. We want girls to be able to access information at all the points of need in their lives as well as to be able to understand situations and make appropriate decisions about what to do next.

I'm reminded of how children learn a first language. We teach phonics, parts of speech, and vocabulary. All the while, however, children are immersed in the language. They hear it spoken, read, and sung. The rhythm, grammar, and syntax become ingrained. Language becomes so much a part of who a child is that she uses it with ease, with confidence, and with fluency. Having absorbed the underlying structures, she can use the language in unpredictable situations automatically, without a prompt on her computer screen.

Our young women need that same confident fluency when they are speaking the language of math and logic, scientific inquiry, artistic expression, literary analysis, or historical exploration. What they learn from a committed school is how to think in the disciplines they are studying. It is not so much the individual bits of information or even the particular skills that are ultimately crucial to being prepared to engage intelligently with the world. Rather, it is the mastery of the range of underlying assumptions, connections, procedures, and logical steps that lets a girl apply these ways of thinking throughout her life.

Not surprisingly, we have similar goals in our nonacademic curriculum, particularly in the ways girls learn to believe in themselves, to be team members, and to act in accordance with their values. What is important is not the little tricks or hints—the "six ways to be in"—of pop culture. Rather, it is learning the grammar and syntax of confidence and competency. Adolescent girls absorb a belief in the value of what they can think and do, the critical importance of their contributions to the world, and the legitimacy of their impulses to lead and to help others.

In guiding girls to learn the underlying structures and principles that will let them find their way successfully and productively in life, we are also seeking to supplant the other curriculum, the one that blares from loudspeakers all around them: Lead with your sexuality. Self-promote. Win at all cost. Providing alternative instruction is not for the faint of heart. Our lessons must be compelling, our approach creative, and our patience inexhaustible. Most importantly, we must build on a girl's authentic self and on her deepest guiding knowledge. In this setting, then, girls will respond by building brave and inspired lives. They will not require point-of-need instructions about life direction and moral choice because they will have become fluent in the syntax of authenticity.

Tips & Tactics

Girls become fluent in being authentic and acting on what they know is right by practicing these behaviors. The next time your daughter tries to mend a relationship with a friend or anticipates having a difficult conversation with a teacher, ask her to practice her lines with you or in front of a mirror. Forming the language and hearing herself say the words will build your daughter's confidence.

76. Privilege with a Cost
Responsibility and Commitment

In a review several years ago of Cristina Rathbone's book *On the Outside Looking In: A Year in an Inner-City High School*, reviewer Stephen O'Connor applauded Rathbone's knack for combining sympathy with realism in her description of the abused but tough kids she befriended. Rathbone's project took her to Manhattan's West Side High School, a facility so strapped financially that students had to share textbooks. O'Connor commented on the "authentic and critically important story" that Rathbone has to tell about these students from poor urban families.[346] What separates the poor from the rest of society, as Rathbone puts it, is "the difference in where we were born and to whom."[347]

I was reminded of a speech I had heard while attending an annual meeting of the National Association of Principals of Schools for Girls. Duke University professor and historian William Chafe spoke of group identity and rights versus individual identity and rights in American society. Throughout our nation's history, the civil rights and women's movements have provided examples of the tension surrounding this issue. The country is committed to the ideal of equal opportunity, but until the very recent decades, according to Chafe, "whether we were born black or white, male or female, rich or poor has totally determined what life chances we have."[348]

From time to time, I speak with girls at Miss Hall's School about privilege. By privilege I do not mean monetary wealth, but rather the privilege every student in the school has just by virtue of the fact that she is here. Peggy McIntosh of the Wellesley Centers for Women, in speaking about the privilege she enjoys because she is white, defines that privilege as "unearned assets . . . [a] weightless knapsack of special provisions, maps, passports, codebooks, visas, clothes, tools, and blank checks."[349] In other words, she was born white and that alone bestows on her advantages.

I remind girls that regardless of whether or not they receive financial aid to attend the school, they are part of a small, select sector of secondary-school students in this country on whom are bestowed great advantages because they are taught by skilled, caring faculty in a nonviolent setting. This quality of education puts them in sharp contrast to many of their peers, particularly when we look globally at the situation for girls and their education. Miss Hall's School students' futures are bright and will be largely of their own making. Our students will go on to matriculate at the finest colleges and universities. Furthermore, their membership in this community connects them to thousands of accomplished alumnae worldwide. Doors will open for these young women; they will have an advantage in society. That is, they have been given provisions for success.

When I talk with our students about the opportunities they have been given, I use the metaphor of being at the table. They are already seated where decisions are being made. Because of this advantage, they will go on to sit at other tables where they will have influence on how society is shaped in this millennium. As we work with our students every day, we look for ways to open their minds and hearts to the sobering work ahead of them. We do not allow them to take their privilege for granted. We continue to teach them that with privilege comes responsibility. We insist that they understand the link between themselves as informed, empowered individuals and the solutions to the multitude of problems facing our society, including hunger, poverty, injustice, lack of medical care, and violence in regions near and far.

The expectation that they have important leadership roles ahead of them needs to be instilled in adolescent girls. In order to assume those roles, they will need to understand how a complex society works and how policy, politics, community structure, and the mass media are related. More importantly, they will have to experience the transformative power of individual involvement and commitment. Teens begin to encounter the complexities of societal structure through a traditional high-school curriculum, but our providing them with an experiential learning opportunity as a parallel teaching method is essential during these years. When a teen can volunteer in organizations vital to a democratic community, she will view issues firsthand and begin to see how she might connect her developing expertise and talent with the work that needs to be done. In other words, through the experience of working with others who are solving complex societal problems, a girl begins to set her own life goals and make an agenda of what she would like to address when she is older.

Girls' understanding of the world is deepened by their awareness that privilege and responsibility go hand in hand. Through traditional study as well as learning experiences that challenge a girl to assume a role in the real world, we make it possible for an adolescent to focus outward, away from self, and toward the large goal of making a difference. By focusing outward in this way, a girl comes to understand how she can best use the privilege she has been given.

Tips & Tactics

Talk with your daughter about the unearned privileges she may have been given because she is . . .

   . . . in a dominant ethnic or religious group.

   . . . the daughter of parents who are committed to her success.

   . . . in a school or neighborhood that is free of violence.

   . . . part of a loving family that provides life's necessities.

   . . . physically and mentally able.

Help her make a list of what she can assume because she was born into her particular circumstance. For example, "I can assume that . . .

... dinner will be provided every evening."

... I won't hear gunshots in my neighborhood."

... I won't have to alter my plans based on wheelchair accessibility."

77. Life Lessons
Conditions for Effective Learning

A t ten, my primary mode of transportation was my bicycle. Although I often walked around the neighborhood, playing with my friends and visiting with neighbors, when I really had a destination or just wanted the adventure of a quick spin around the block, my bike was it. On one such trip, I rounded the corner at Pennsylvania and 21st Streets and started the block-long, exhilarating downhill run toward 20th Street, a main east-west thoroughfare through Joplin. As I picked up speed, ponytail flying, I was aware of the cars zooming by on the busy road ahead. Whether I was caught up in the thrill of the ride or had let my mind wonder, I don't know. What I do remember is that by the time it occurred to me that I should start to brake to avoid sailing out into the oncoming traffic, it was too late. Sail I did, right into the fender of a car, which fortunately was not moving. The driver had seen me coming and minimized the crash by stopping.

I managed to avoid bike disaster for the remainder of my childhood. A few years later, however, as a new driver of automobiles who had learned nothing about Newton's laws of motion from that scary bike trip, I misgauged the time needed to stop and slid into the bumper of the car ahead of me, tires screeching. I had been driving down Joplin Street to pick up my dad from work, so his tune-up talk about judging distances and the time needed to slow down came almost instantaneously. With that lesson, I was convinced that I had to start paying attention to what was in front of me. I began to improve.

I have daily opportunities to reflect on the conditions that create effective learning. Effective learning has to do with our taking what we have been taught and applying it successfully to new situations. As we parent and teach teens, it is good to reflect on how we learned our own life lessons, in bicycling and beyond. Since life is the great classroom, every experience an adolescent girl encounters provides an opportunity for her to refine what she has learned earlier. Her expertise grows as she successfully deals with new circumstances. Indeed, she finds that outcomes become increasingly more positive as she gains confidence, applies new skills, takes full advantage of her strengths, and hones the strategies she has devised to offset abilities that may be less strong than others.

To accelerate this process, as educators we encourage girls to reflect on their accomplishments and to identify the techniques they used that made those accomplishments possible. Being reflective is a skill we want them to develop throughout their adolescent years and beyond. Whether we are fifteen or fifty, we benefit when we ask ourselves certain questions: What did I do to create this success? What help did I receive from others? What could I have done differently to avoid disappointment? What strategies have worked before that I should have applied here? Recently, I saw a student essay in which the author described new insight into her approach to studying. She wrote, "As a result of this knowledge, I have started to use my strengths . . . and am better in integrating all my resources." This student exhibited keen insight into her learning, and this level of awareness is a key factor in human intelligence.

Cognitive psychologist Robert J. Sternberg has put forth several influential learning theories in his career. The most groundbreaking is his triarchic theory of successful intelligence, in which he defines intelligent people as "those who have the ability to achieve success according to their own definition of success, within their sociocultural context."[350] They do this, he says, "by identifying and capitalizing on their strengths and identifying and correcting or compensating for their weaknesses."[351] The essential aspect of Sternberg's work in relation to dealing with teens, however, is that he views intelligence "as a form of developing competencies, and competencies as forms of developing expertise. . . . In other words, intelligence is modifiable rather than fixed."[352]

Whether an adolescent girl is analyzing data in a statistics course or trying to figure out why she and her roommate had a falling out, she is developing competency. That competency will lead to deep expertise in whichever areas of endeavor she has chosen to pursue. Our job as parents and as teachers is to inspire girls to engage fully in experience-rich environments, to reflect on their performances, to develop their talents, to compensate for their weaknesses, and to enjoy the smart and accomplished young women they are becoming.

Every year I read to students Portia Nelson's poem, "Autobiography in Five Short Chapters," from her book *There's a Hole in My Sidewalk: The Romance of Self-Discovery*.[353] Nelson's metaphor delivers the message that when we engage, reflect, and adjust, success can be ours.

"Autobiography in Five Short Chapters"

Chapter One
    I walk down the street.
    There is a deep hole in the sidewalk.
    I fall in.
    I am lost . . . I am hopeless.
    It isn't my fault.
    It takes forever to find a way out.

Chapter Two
    I walk down the same street.
    There is a deep hole in the sidewalk.
    I pretend I don't see it.
    I fall in again.
    I can't believe I'm in the same place.
    But, it isn't my fault.
    It still takes a long time to get out.

Chapter Three

>I walk down the same street.
>
>There is a deep hole in the sidewalk.
>
>I *see* it is there.
>
>I still fall in . . . it's a habit . . . but,
>
>my eyes are open.
>
>I know where I am.
>
>It is *my* fault.
>
>I get out immediately.

Chapter Four

>I walk down the same street.
>
>There is a deep hole in the sidewalk.
>
>I walk around it.

Chapter Five

>I walk down another street.

Tips & Tactics

Girls can be quick to attribute their success to luck. It is important, therefore, to help them understand the role they play in their achievements. Look for opportunities to ask your daughter how she was able to earn an A on a test, win the election, or score points in the game. What personal qualities contributed to her success? What did she have to overcome? Did she enlist the support of others? This type of reflection helps her to see her own resourcefulness.

78. Quality of Life
The Value of Happiness

Now well into her nineties, my mom still refers to our small house in Joplin, Missouri, as "Grand Central Station." By that she means that it was a gathering place. I remember as a child growing up there that people frequently stopped by, whether to stay and chat or just to breeze through on their way to someplace else. Located one block off Main Street, our house was easily on the way to many places in my hometown. Neighbors walked over, the preacher would drop in as he was making his rounds, and friends from other parts of town were always wheeling into the driveway. I got used to the everyday presence of a collection of folks, coming through the side door, standing around, sitting down at the kitchen table, drinking coffee, laughing, talking. Many nights as a child, I fell asleep to the happy hum of visitors.

Security, connection, and belonging wrapped around my childhood, and if those feelings of well-being could have been contained in a box and sold in a happiness store, my parents' bank account would have grown. Their wealth, however, was best measured in capital that was more than financial. According to an article in the *New York Times* by Andrew Revkin, some world economists are beginning to think that the wealth of a country might best be measured the same way, by calculating not just its gross domestic product (GDP) but also how happy and content its citizens are.[354]

A few years ago, four hundred people representing over a dozen countries met in Nova Scotia, as Revkin writes, "to consider new ways to define and assess prosperity."[355] Sharing their experience of measuring "gross national happiness" were representatives from the tiny Himalayan nation of Bhutan, a country that decided back in the early seventies to focus on citizens' well-being instead of its GDP. Admittedly, Bhutan's example, says Revkin, is still "a work in progress," but the concept of thinking of public welfare in ways that are broader than economics alone is being considered by a number of world economists, social scientists, and corporate and government leaders.[356] Focusing only on economic expansion ignores quality-of-life factors that should be considered, as progress and happiness are about more than bottom-line growth.

There is a parallel version of this issue in education. At Miss Hall's School, we have a robust vision for girls' education. Our program is broad, sophisticated, and designed to inspire girls to grow in myriad ways, many of them nonquantifiable. College admission offices, however, look at a relatively narrow range of factors, most of which can be reduced to a few numbers, to assess applicants. Furthermore, schools and colleges are vulnerable to outside assessments that include too few pieces. As we know, the news media is only too happy to rank schools based on a handful of figures that don't begin to reflect the depth of our institutions.

Given the prevalence in the culture for using shorthand markers of success, schools themselves need to guard against defining their prowess in narrow terms. Just as growth and success for countries should include factors beyond consumer expenditures and business investments, a school's scorecard should go beyond quantifiable outcomes to include how students perceive their daily experiences. Recently I sat down in my office with a few students and asked them to explain why visiting families often comment on the level of happiness at the school. One girl said, "It's the sense of community; we know each other's names. We have a connection, which in itself encourages us to resolve our problems." Another added, "We're comfortable here, and that leads to being happy." The affirming approach that teachers use was also mentioned. One student said, "You just feel supported, cheered on. If you fail in one thing, you just move ahead because you know there are many more places where you'll succeed."

The girls also discussed how being heard shapes their experiences. The student body had just finished a successful eighteen-month process to change the school's cell phone policy, and the rush that accompanied that achievement was still with them. One girl said, "I just feel that I can accomplish my goals after Miss Hall's." I asked her to explain, and she added, "Well, if I'm listened to here, I'll be listened to out there."

We measure the success of this school not by the pace of the race to a thin finish line but by the quality of a girl's experience. Security, connection, and belonging wrap around the students here, and I would like to think that because of that, the next generation of leaders presently being educated at Miss Hall's School will help us imagine a better world.

Tips & Tactics

In order for your daughter to develop confidence in her own voice, she must know that others are listening to her. Ask her if she believes she is being heard in her school. Where does she have the chance to speak her mind and to work with others to effect change? If your daughter's school is not providing these opportunities, identify other venues where she can have these experiences.

79. What Dreams Are Made Of
Raising Girls' Expectations

I dreamed of being Miss America or Doris Day. Either one would have been fine. Every September Bert Parks sang, "There she is . . . ," and I imagined myself walking down the runway as Miss America, waving to the crowd, balancing the tiara perfectly on my head. Doris Day was the other option. Well, not actually Doris Day, but the characters she played in the movies. Mostly wives and mothers, they fit generally with the preset role I was to assume when the time came. Day's portrayals, however, offered pluck and professionalism along with pearls and pacifiers. Gorgeously dressed, beautifully coiffed, the women that Day inhabited were strong-willed, independent (up to a point), and outspoken.

Except in movies, combining family and career was not the stuff dreams were made of when I was a teen. Female athletes, doctors, or business executives were not anywhere I was. Role models who could have inspired me to think about what was possible were limited, and I didn't meet female heroes and writers when I opened books at school. The dedication and attentiveness from my teachers stopped just short of communicating the aspiration that would have inspired me to dream big.

A *Forbes Magazine* article recently caught my eye with the title "Close the Gender Gap and Dream Big." It reported on research findings that reveal the 27 percent revenue gap between women-owned businesses and those owned by men.[357] Maxine Clark, the founder of the highly successful Build-A-Bear Workshop, is quoted as saying that women are "not dreaming big enough."[358] Renee Martin, the article's author, characterizes Clark as a woman whose confidence allowed her to "shoot for the stars" and avoid limiting her dreams to suit others' lowered expectations.[359] What the research concluded was that the revenue gap has developed in part because of women's own self-limiting views of what they are capable of, the fear of failure, and the lack of the relationship building needed to leverage potential.[360]

The factors identified as limiting growth in start-up companies are similar to the factors that often limit our young women as they start up their lives. Learning how to dream big, to take healthy risks, to fail and recover, and to expand one's influence through networking are essential skills, and the optimum time to learn and practice them is in the high-school years. It is between the ages of thirteen and eighteen that a girl is cognitively and psychologically ready to engage with new and expansive ideas about the world and her place in it. Our job, as parents and teachers, is to challenge her to make the most of that readiness.

Each fall when ninth graders enter Miss Hall's School, they begin to reflect on what it means to lead. That is, they begin the conversation about how one sets personal goals, finds ways to achieve them, and works with others to create change. As girls talk, we begin to hear their apprehensions. Do I think I'll run for office? (I might lose the election.) Could I describe something I am passionate about? (Others might think it's silly.) Could I meet with a teacher to ask for help with an assignment? (She might think I'm stupid.) In other words, the brakes start to go on, and a girl begins to contemplate playing it safe rather than taking the risks that allow her to become competent and in charge of her life.

Playing it safe is about a girl wanting to control others' responses to what she says and does. It is about avoiding disapproval from peers and adults. The problem, of course, with focusing so intensely on others' reactions is that a girl's dreams begin to shrink to fit the narrow lens through which she is now viewing the world. As parents and educators, our work with girls is to prevent that from happening.

As students begin a new year, they learn the skills they need to exercise their personal authority, develop resilience, and risk failure. Freshwomen thinking about running for office attend student council meetings in small groups to observe older girls in action and to join in on discussions. Senior proctors wanting to discharge their duties but worried about causing upset discuss and then practice the best language to use when the goal is to support *and* to clarify. Risks taken. Goals accomplished. Confidence built.

We know that it takes a few years for a girl to progress from beginning algebra to calculus. In like manner, it takes time for a girl to learn how to move beyond worrying what others will think to considering whether she is being true to herself and honest about her goals. Our job as teachers and parents is never to let an opportunity for learning slip by. Every time we give a girl the tools she needs to step out of her comfort zone, we are making it possible for her to increase her chances for success. That *is* the stuff dreams are made of.

Tips & Tactics

Look for signs that your daughter is playing it safe, rather than taking the healthy risks that will allow her to grow and learn. Talk with her about her wildest dreams. If anything were possible, what would she like to be doing artistically? Academically? Athletically? In her community? Then ask her what prevents her from working toward those goals. During the teen years, many girls need permission from parents and teachers to dream big. Give that permission to your daughter.

Notes

1. Works in Progress

1   National Institute of Mental Health, *Teenage Brain: A Work in Progress (Fact Sheet)*, NIH publication no. 01-4929, accessed August 4, 2011, http://www.nimh.nih.gov/health/publications/teenage-brain-a-work-in-progress-fact-sheet/index.shtml.
2   Ibid.
3   Ann Barnet and Richard Barnet, "Childcare Brain Drain? (White House Conference on Early Childhood Focuses on Importance of Early Years in Developing Brain Structure)," Editorial, *Nation*, May 12, 1997, 6; Gail Lindsey, "Brain Research and Implications for Early Childhood Education," *Childhood Education*, Winter 1998, 97.
4   Sharon Begley, "Mind Expansion: Inside the Teenage Brain," *Newsweek*, May 8, 2000, 68.

2. Authentic Character Building

5   David Brooks, "'Moral Suicide,' à la Wolfe," review of *I Am Charlotte Simmons*, by Tom Wolfe, *New York Times*, November 16, 2004.
6   Ibid.
7   Elizabeth Debold, Marie C. Wilson, and Idelisse Malavé, *Mother Daughter Revolution: From Betrayal to Power* (Reading, MA: Addison-Wesley, 1993), 177.
8   Brooks, "'Moral Suicide,' à la Wolfe."

3. The Challenge to Be Oneself

9   David Elkind, *All Grown Up and No Place to Go: Teenagers in Crisis* (Reading, MA: Addison-Wesley, 1989), 164.
10 Ibid.
11 Ibid., 164-165.
12 Ibid., 165.

5. A Life in Reflection

13 Donald A. Schön, *The Reflective Practitioner: How Professionals Think in Action* (New York: Basic Books, 1983), 8.

14 Ibid., 9.

15 Donald A. Schön, "Preparing Professionals for the Demands of Practice," in *Educating the Reflective Practitioner: Toward a New Design for Teaching and Learning in the Professions* (San Francisco: Jossey-Bass, 1987), 3-21.

16 Ibid., 4.

17 Ibid.

18 Ibid., 22.

19 Ibid., 26.

20 Schön, *The Reflective Practioner*, 50.

21 Schön, "The Dialogue between Coach and Student," in *Educating the Reflective Practitioner*, 100-118.

6. Taking the Lead

22 Nannerl O. Keohane, "Update on Duke's Women's Initiative," *Duke News and Communications*, April 25, 2003, http://dukespace.lib.duke.edu/dspace/bitstream/10161/1546/1/NOK20030424.pdf.

23 Steering Committee on Undergraduate Women's Leadership at Princeton, *Report of the Steering Committee on Undergraduate Women's Leadership: Summary of Findings and Recommendations*, Princeton University Reports, March 2011, 4, http://www.princeton.edu/reports/2011/leadership/.

24 Ibid., 6.

25 Ibid.

26 Ibid., 9.

27 Ibid.

28 Ibid.

7. Talking the Talk

29 Jill McLean Taylor, Carol Gilligan, and Amy Sullivan, *Between Voice and Silence: Women and Girls, Race and Relationships* (Cambridge, MA.: Harvard University Press, 1995), 3.

30 Peggy Orenstein, *Schoolgirls: Young Women, Self-Esteem, and the Confidence Gap* (New York: Doubleday, 1994), 36.

8. Can We Talk?

31 Mary Pipher, *The Shelter of Each Other: Rebuilding Our Families* (New York: G. P. Putnam's Sons, 1996), 138.

9. Essential Rebellion

32 Sara Rimer, "A 'Rebellious Daughter' to Lead Harvard," *New York Times*, February 12, 2007.

33 "Drew Gilpin Faust '68 to Lead Harvard," *Bryn Mawr Now*, February 11, 2007, http://www.brynmawr.edu/news/2007-02-11/faust.shtml.

34 Rimer, "A 'Rebellious Daughter' to Lead Harvard."

35 Ibid.

10. When No One Is Watching

36 Kevin Ryan and Karen Bohlin, "Values, Views, or Virtues?," *Education Week*, March 3, 1999, 49, 72.

37 Carol Tauer, e-mail message to author, June 27, 2011.

38 Ibid.

39 Ibid.

11. The Patience Fuse

40 Ann Pleshette Murphy and Jennifer Allen, "Inside the Teenage Brain," *Good Morning America*, ABCNews, July 31, 2006, http://abcnews.go.com/GMA/AmericanFamily/story?id=2248295&page=1.

41 Ibid.

42 Ibid.

12. Step by Step

43 Anne Marie Chaker, "Schools Face Up to Reality: Mom Is Doing the Homework," *Wall Street*

Journal, October 29, 2002.

44 Ibid.

45 *Webster's New World College Dictionary*, 4th ed., s.v. "process."

13. Girl Talk

46 Sarah Kershaw, "Girl Talk Has Its Limits," *New York Times*, September 11, 2008.

47 Ibid.

48 Ibid.

49 Ibid.

14. Eye to Eye

50 Louann Brizendine, *The Female Brain* (New York: Broadway Books, 2006), 120-121.

51 Ibid., 17.

52 Ibid., 33.

53 Annie Dillard, *The Maytrees* (New York: Harper Perennial, 2008), 7.

54 Susan Scott, *Fierce Conversations: Achieving Success in Work and Life, One Conversation at a Time* (New York: Berkley Books, 2004), 6.

55 Ibid., 199.

15. Cranky Chronicles

56 Emily Nussbaum, "My So-Called Blog," *New York Times*, January 11, 2004.

57 Rachel Simmons, *Odd Girl Out: The Hidden Culture of Aggression in Girls* (New York: Harcourt, 2002) 17.

58 Peggy Orenstein, *Schoolgirls*, 37.

59 Simmons, *Odd Girl Out*, 115.

16. The Tangled Web We Weave

60 "Babies Learn to Lie Before They Talk," *Times of India*, July 10, 2007, http://articles.timesofindia.indiatimes.com/2007-07-10/science/27955000_1_babies-infants-eye-contact.

61 Richard Gray, "Babies Not as Innocent as They Pretend," *Telegraph* (UK), July 1, 2007, http://www.telegraph.co.uk/earth/main.jhtml?xml=/earth/2007/07/01/scibaby101.xml.

62 Richard W. Byrne and Andrew Whiten, "Machiavellian Intelligence," in *Machiavellian Intelligence II: Extensions and Evaluations*, ed. Andrew Whiten and Richard W. Bryne (Cambridge, UK: Cambridge University Press, 1997), 1, http://catdir.loc.gov/catdir/samples/cam031/96048233.pdf.

63 Ibid.

64 Ibid., 2.

65 "Babies Learn to Lie Before They Talk."

66 Ibid.

17. May I Help You?

67 Daniel Goleman, *Emotional Intelligence: Why It Can Matter More Than IQ* (New York: Bantam Books, 1995), 98.

68 Ibid., 96.

69 Ibid.

70 Ibid.

71 Ibid.

72 William Shakespeare, *Hamlet*, in *The Yale Shakespeare*, ed. Wilbur L. Cross and Tucker Brooke (New York: Barnes and Noble, 2005), act 3, scene 1, lines 69-70.

73 "Difference between Justice and Charity," DifferenceBetween, accessed August 4, 2011, http://www.differencebetween.net/language/difference-between-justice-and-charity/.

18. Just Like Us

74 "Selected Characteristics of People at Specified Levels of Poverty in the Past Twelve Months,"

in *2006-2009 American Community Survey Three-Year Estimates*, US Census Bureau, accessed August 4, 2011, http://factfinder.census.gov/servlet/STTable?_bm=y&-geo_id=01000US&-qr_name=ACS_2009_3YR_G00_S1703&-ds_name=ACS_2009_3YR_G00_&-_lang=en&-redoLog=false&-format=&-CONTEXT=st; "Domestic Sex Trafficking of Minors," in *Child Prostitution*, US Department of Justice, Criminal Division, Child Exploitation and Obscenity Section, accessed August 4, 2011, http://www.justice.gov/criminal/ceos/prostitution.html.

75   "Women's Rights Division," Human Rights Watch, accessed August 4, 2011, http://www.hrw.org/en/node/82134.

19. She's Got High Hopes

76   Carol Christ, "Their Moment in History," *Smith Alumnae Quarterly*, Winter 2007-2008, 18.

77   Ibid., 19.

78   "Latest Catalyst Census Shows Women Still Not Scaling the Corporate Ladder in 2010; New Study Indicates Clue to Reversing Trend," Catalyst, December 13, 2010, http://www.catalyst.org/press-release/181/latest-catalyst-census-shows-women-still-not-scaling-the-corporate-ladder-in-2010-new-study-indicates-clue-to-reversing-trend.

20. Success with Integrity

79   Ellen Goodman, "The Mythology of Rosa Parks," *Boston Globe*, October 28, 2005.

80   Ibid.

81   Ibid.

82   Ibid.

83   Stephanie Armour, "Do Women Compete in Unhealthy Ways at Work?," *USA Today*, December 29, 2005.

84   Ibid.

85   Ibid.

86   Ibid.

21. The Double Bind

87   Angela Shah, "Zen and the Art of a New Career," *The National* (Abu Dhabi, UAE), June 30, 2009, http://www.thenational.ae/article/20090630/BUSINESS/706309914/1396.

88   Masha Jones, Editorial, Miss Hall's School's *Hallways*, March 2007.

89   Erin White, "Advice for Women on Developing a Leadership Style," *Wall Street Journal*, August 28, 2007.

90   Ibid.

91   Ibid.

92   Ibid.

93   Carol Gilligan, Nona P. Lyons, and Trudy J. Hanmer, eds., *Making Connections: The Relational Worlds of Adolescent Girls at Emma Willard School* (New York: Emma Willard School, 1989), 85.

94   Ibid.

22. Voice Lessons

95   Catharine MacKinnon, "Now More Than Ever," *Smith Alumnae Quarterly*, Winter 2009-2010, 45.

96   Ibid.

97   "Madeline K. Albright's Commencement Address to the Wellesley College Class of 2007," Wellesley College Office for Public Affairs, http://www.wellesley.edu/PublicAffairs/Commencement/2007/MAlbright.html.

98   Ibid.

99   Josie Amadeo, e-mail correspondence with the author, August 31, 2010.

100   "Hayley McFarland on Verizon Commercial," Metacafe, accessed August 4, 2011, http://www.metacafe.com/watch/5088003/hayley_mcfarland_on_verizon_commercial/.

23. Who's in Charge?

101   Daniel Zalewski, "The Defiant Ones," *New Yorker*, October 19, 2009, http://www.newyorker.

com/arts/critics/atlarge/2009/10/19/091019crat_atlarge_zalewski?currentPage=all.

102   Ibid.

103   Ibid.

104   Bonnie Harris, "You're Not the Worst Parent in the World!," Monadnock Action Network with Youth (MANY), accessed August 4, 2011, http://www.monadnockparents.org/teens-today/you%E2%80%99re-not-worst-parent-world.

105   Ibid.

106   Bonnie Harris, "The Power Struggle," *Bonnie Harris Connective Parenting Newsletter*, November 2009, http://www.bonnieharris.com/news1109.html.

107   Bonnie Harris, "Too Involved or Not Involved Enough?," *Monadnock Ledger-Transcript*, February 2005, http://www.bonnieharris.com/columns/0205.pdf.

24. Free-Range Education

108   Wendy Mogel, *The Blessing of a Skinned Knee: Using Jewish Teachings to Raise Self-Reliant Children* (New York: Penguin Compass, 2001), 96.

109   Nancy Gibbs, "The Growing Backlash against Overparenting," *Time*, November 20, 2009, http://www.time.com/time/magazine/article/0,9171,1940697,00.html.

110   Ibid.

111   Philip K. Howard, *The Death of Common Sense: How Law Is Suffocating America* (New York: Warner Books, 1994), 5.

112   Ibid., 1.

25. Predicting Happiness

113   John Gertner, "The Futile Pursuit of Happiness," *New York Times Magazine*, September 7, 2003, http://www.nytimes.com/2003/09/07/magazine/the-futile-pursuit-of-happiness.html.

114   Ibid.

115   Ibid.

116   Ibid.

117   Ibid.

118   Ibid.

26. Community Life

119   Nancy Gibbs et al., "Parents and Children: Who's in Charge Here?," *Time*, August 6, 2001, http://www.time.com/time/magazine/article/0,9171,1000465-1,00.html.

120   Ibid.

121   Ibid.

122   Ruth Simmons, "My Mother's Daughter: Lessons I Learned in Civility and Authenticity," *Texas Journal of Ideas, History, and Culture*, Spring/Summer 1998, and reprinted in *College Board Review*, May 2001, 9.

27. School Clothes and Life

123   Olivia Barker, "School Shopping Goes Pro," *USA Today*, August 23, 2004.

124   Ibid.

125   Ibid.

28. A Special Case

126   Polly Young-Eisendrath, *The Self-Esteem Trap: Raising Confident and Compassionate Kids in an Age of Self-Importance* (New York: Little, Brown, 2008), 32, 33.

127   Ibid., 48.

128   Max Roosevelt, "Student Expectations Seen as Causing Grade Disputes," *New York Times*, February 18, 2009.

129   Ibid.

130   Ibid.

131   Ibid.

132   Ibid.

29. You're the Top

133   Christie Mellor, *The Three-Martini Playdate: A Practical Guide to Happy Parenting* (San Francisco: Chronicle Books, 2004), 114.
134   Ibid.
135   Ibid.
136   Ibid., 115.
137   Michael Riera, "The Hidden Logic of Students in Everyday Life" (lecture, annual meeting of the National Association of Principals of Schools for Girls, Rancho Bernardo, CA, March 2, 2005), http://www.napsg.org/riera05.htm.
138   Ibid.

30. Never Home Alone

139   Jane Adams, "The Kids Aren't All Right," *Smith Alumnae Quarterly*, Spring 2004, 24.
140   Ibid., 27, 24.
141   Ibid., 26.
142   Ibid.
143   William Aquilino, "Family Relationships and Support Systems in Emerging Adulthood" (paper, Conference on Emerging Adulthood, Harvard University, Cambridge, MA, November 2003).

31. That's Life!

144   Sue Shellenbarger, "It's Not about You: The Emotional Toll of Being Too Involved in Your Kid's Life," *Wall Street Journal*, April 14, 2005.
145   Ibid.
146   Ibid.
147   Ibid.

33. Eyes on the Prize

148   William Damon, *Greater Expectations: Overcoming the Culture of Indulgence in Our Homes and Schools* (New York: Free Press, 1995), 22.
149   Ibid., 16.

35. Lighten Up

150   David Anderegg, *Worried All the Time: Overparenting in an Age of Anxiety and How to Stop It* (New York: Free Press, 2003), 2.
151   Ibid., 26.

37. A Life of One's Own

152   Iona Opie and Peter Opie, *The Lore and Language of Children* (New York: New York Review of Books, 2001), x.
153   Ibid., xiv.
154   Carl Jung, "The Development of Personality," in *Collected Works* (Princeton, NJ: Princeton University Press, 1954), vol. 17, par. 295.
155   Sam Schulman, "Letting Go," *Wall Street Journal*, March 3, 2006.
156   Ibid.
157   Ibid.

38. On the Road Again

158   Tina Kelly, "Dear Parents: Please Relax, It's Just Camp," *New York Times*, July 26, 2008.
159   Pipher, *The Shelter of Each Other*, 224.
160   Ibid.
161   Kelly, "Dear Parents."
162   Maryann Rosenthal, *Be a Parent, Not a Pushover: A Guide to Raising Happy, Emotionally Healthy Teens* (Nashville, TN: Nelson Books, 2006), 118.

163 Ibid., 117.
164 Ibid.

39. Less Is More
165 David Cudaback, e-mail correspondence with the author, April 4, 2008.

40. Gunsmoke in the Garage
166 Sharon Begley, "Pink Brain, Blue Brain: Claims of Sex Differences Fall Apart," review of *Pink Brain, Blue Brain: How Small Differences Grow into Troublesome Gaps—and What We Can Do about It*, by Lise Eliot, *Newsweek*, September 3, 2009, http://www.thedailybeast.com/newsweek/2009/09/02/pink-brain-blue-brain.html.
167 Ibid.
168 Associated Press, "Study: Women Create 'Their Own Glass Ceiling,'" Careers, Msnbc, August 10, 2009, http://www.msnbc.msn.com/id/32364451/ns/business-careers/.
169 Ibid.

41. The Tallest Oak
170 Malcolm Gladwell, *Outliers: The Story of Success* (New York: Little, Brown, 2008), 104.
171 Ibid., 105.
172 Ibid., 102, 101.
173 Ibid., 79.
174 Ibid., 80.
175 Ibid., 11.
176 David Brooks, "Lost in the Crowd," *New York Times*, December 16, 2008.
177 Gladwell, *Outliers*, 105.
178 Ibid., 19.
179 Ibid., 113.
180 Hillary Fitch, e-mail correspondence with the author, October 20, 2008.

43. Dale Evans Revisited
181 Kathy Grannis, "Though Electronics Remain Popular, Low-Priced Toys Are Tops This Holiday Season," National Retail Federation, November 20, 2009, http://www.nrf.com/modules.php?name=News&op=viewlive&sp_id=834; "Games and Activities for Girls," Mattel, accessed August 4, 2011, http://www.barbie.com.
182 "Fisher-Price Boys," Fisher-Price, accessed August 4, 2011, http://www.fisher-price.com/uk/boys.asp; "Unique Toys for Girls at Fisher-Price," Fisher-Price, accessed August 4, 2011, http://www.fisher-price.com/fp.aspx?st=10&e=girlslanding.
183 "Joycelyn Elders Quotes," Brainy Quote, accessed August 4, 2011, http://www.brainyquote.com/quotes/authors/j/joycelyn_elders.html.

44. Have Some Potatoes
184 Jeffrey Zaslow, "Out of Line: Why We're Reluctant to Reprimand Other People's Children," *Wall Street Journal*, July 27, 2006.
185 Ibid.
186 Ibid.
187 Pipher, *The Shelter of Each Other*, 9.
188 Ibid., 224.

45. Remember When?
189 Sue Shellenbarger, "When Fond Memories from Your Kids' Past Don't Even Ring a Bell," *Wall Street Journal*, October 28, 1998.
190 Ibid.
191 Ibid.
192 Ibid.
193 Ibid.

46. Powerful Ideas

194   Walt Whitman, "Song of Myself," in *The Portable Walt Whitman*, ed. Mark Van Doren (New York: Viking Press, 1953), 67.

195   Stephanie Steinberg, "Teen Girls Say Kids More Likely to Drink, Do Drugs to Cope," *USA Today*, June 29, 2010.

196   "Research Brief: Teenage Girls Increasingly Vulnerable to Alcohol and Drug Use," Partnership for a Drug-Free America, 2009, http://www.somethingdigital-wp.com/drugfree/wp-content/uploads/2010/09/Brief-Special_Analysis_on_Teen_Girls.pdf.

197   Ibid.

198   Mayo Clinic Staff, "Teen Drinking: Talking to Your Teen about Alcohol," Tween and Teen Health, Mayo Clinic, April 23, 2011, http://www.mayoclinic.com/health/teen-drinking/MY00521.

199   J. J. Sabia, "Does Early Adolescent Sex Cause Depressive Symptoms?," Abstract, National Center for Biotechnology Information, US National Library of Medicine, National Institutes of Health, Fall 2006, http://www.ncbi.nlm.nih.gov/pubmed/16989034.

47. Leading with the Mind

200   "Number of Sexual Scenes on TV Nearly Double Since 1998," Kaiser Family Foundation, November 9, 2005, http://www.kff.org/entmedia/entmedia110905nr.cfm.

201   Valerie Horres, "Boobs or Bitches: The Way the Internet Portrays Women," *Interface: The Journal of Education, Community, and Values*, December 2009, http://bcis.pacificu.edu/journal/article.php?id=621.

202   American Psychological Association, Task Force on the Sexualization of Girls, *Report of the APA Task Force on the Sexualization of Girls* (Washington, DC: American Psychological Association, 2010), 13, http://www.apa.org/pi/women/programs/girls/report-full.pdf.

203   Sherrill Sellman, "The Problem of Precocious Puberty," *Nexus Magazine* (Aus.), April-May 2004, 1, 2, http://www.oasisadvancedwellness.com/learning/precocious-puberty.html.

204   Lynn Ponton, *The Romance of Risk: Why Teenagers Do the Things They Do* (New York: Basic Books, 1997), 72.

205   American Psychological Association, Task Force on the Sexualization of Girls, *Report of the APA Task Force*, 2.

206   Deborah Roffman, "Dangerous Games: A Sex Video Broke the Rules, but for Kids the Rules Have Changed," *Washington Post*, April 15, 2001.

207   Deborah Roffman, *Sex and Sensibility: The Thinking Parent's Guide to Talking Sense about Sex* (Cambridge, MA: Perseus Books, 2001), 4.

48. The Objective Case

208   Diane E. Levin and Jean Kilbourne, *So Sexy, So Soon: The New Sexualized Childhood and What Parents Can Do to Protect Their Kids* (New York: Ballantine Books, 2008), 178.

209   Ibid., 155.

210   Ibid., 156.

211   Scott A. Lukas, "The Gender Ads Project," Gender Ads, accessed August 5, 2011, http://www.genderads.com./Gender_Ads.com.html.

49. Resisting Media Messages

212   James P. Steyer, *The Other Parent: The Inside Story of the Media's Effect on Our Children* (New York: Atria Books, 2002), 55.

213   Ibid., 94.

214   Jackson Katz and Sut Jhally, "The National Conversation in the Wake of Littleton Is Missing the Mark," *Boston Globe*, May 2, 1999.

215   Ibid.

50. Aesop for Girls

216   William Safire, "Aesop's Fabled Fox," *New York Times*, December 29, 2003.

51. Balancing the Scale

217   Catherine Steiner-Adair, "Mind, Body, and Spirit: Caring for Girls within Our Care" (keynote address summary, annual meeting of the National Coalition of Girls' Schools, Madeira School, McLean, VA, June 26-28, 1995).

218   Ibid.

219   *Beauty at Any Cost: A YWCA Report on the Consequences of America's Beauty Obsession on Women and Girls*, YWCA USA, August 18, 2008, 2, http://www.ywca.org/atf/cf/%7B3B450FA5-108B-4D2E-B3D0-C31487243E6A%7D/Beauty%20at%20Any%20Cost.pdf.

220   "A 5' 4" Average American Female," WonderQuest, accessed August 5, 2011, http://www.wonderquest.com/size-women-us.htm.

221   "SoYouWanna Be a Model?," SoYouWanna, accessed August 5, 2011, http://www.soyouwanna.com/site/syws/model/model.html.

222   Steiner-Adair, "Mind, Body and Spirit."

223   Ibid.

52. Rites of Passage

224   Monique P. Yazigi, "A Sweet-16-Going-on-25 Party," *New York Times*, February 7, 1999.

225   Marian Wright Edelman, "Standing Up for the World's Children: Leave No Child Behind" (circa 1996), Gifts of Speech, accessed August 5, 2011, http://gos.sbc.edu/e/edelman.html.

226   Yazigi, "A Sweet-16-Going-on-25 Party."

227   Ibid.

228   "Sex, Drugs, and Rock and Roll: Do Parents Influence Teen Behavior?," Moving Traditions, accessed August 5, 2011, http://www.movingtraditions.org/index.php?option=com_content&task=view&id=16&Itemid=30.

53. The Perils of Popularity

229   Rachel Simmons, *Odd Girl Out*, 156.

230   Ibid., 159.

231   Ibid., 156.

232   Society for Research in Child Development, "The Dark Side of Adolescent Popularity," *ScienceDaily*, May 17, 2005, http://www.sciencedaily.com/releases/2005/05/050517143704.htm.

233   Ibid.

234   Benedict Carey, "Spot on Popularity Scale Speaks to the Future; Middle Has Its Rewards," *New York Times*, September 1, 2008.

235   Society for Research in Child Development, "The Dark Side of Adolescent Popularity."

54. The Need to Belong

236   Pat Wingert and Barbara Kantrowitz, "How Well Do You Know Your Kid?," *Newsweek*, May 10, 1999, http://www.newsweek.com/1999/05/09/how-well-do-you-know-your-kid.html.

237   Ibid.

238   Joan Jacobs Brumberg, *The Body Project: An Intimate History of American Girls* (New York: Vintage Books, 1998), xix-xx.

239   Stephen S. Hall, "The Troubled Life of Boys: The Bully in the Mirror," *New York Times Magazine*, August 22, 1999, http://www.nytimes.com/1999/08/22/magazine/the-troubled-life-of-boys-the-bully-in-the-mirror.html?scp=1&sq=troubled%20life%20of%20boys&st=cse.

55. Old-Fashioned Girls

240   Jeffrey Zaslow, "The End of Youthful Indiscretions," *Wall Street Journal*, August 12, 2004.

241   Ibid.

242   "American Awful," Editorial, *New York Times*, January 23, 2005.

243   Ibid.

56. No Proof Needed

244   Laura O. Palmer, "An Interview with Jan Civian, Project Director [of the Pathways for Women

in the Sciences Project, Part II]," *Research Report*, Spring 1996, 3.

245   Peggy Orenstein, "Why Science Must Adapt to Women," *Discover*, November 2002, http://discovermagazine.com/2002/nov/featadapt.

246   Ibid.

247   Ibid.

248   Ibid.

249   Ibid.

250   Ibid.

251   Ibid.

252   Ibid.

253   Ibid.

254   Mary Pipher, *Reviving Ophelia: Saving the Selves of Adolescent Girls* (New York: G. P. Putnam's Sons, 1994), 22.

57. Effortless Perfection

255   Sam Hull, "The Women's Initiative Rolls On," *Duke Today*, October 31, 2007, http://news.duke.edu/2007/10/alumni.html.

256   Ibid.

257   Melinda Barlow, "Abolishing 'Effortless Perfection,'" National Education Association, accessed August 5, 2011, http://www.nea.org/home/34818.htm.

258   Lisa Belkin, "The Feminine Critique," *New York Times*, November 1, 2007.

259   Ibid.

260   Ibid.

261   Ibid.

58. Imperfect Perfection

262   Sara Rimer, "For Girls, It's Be Yourself, and Be Perfect, Too," *New York Times*, April 1, 2007.

263   Ibid.

264   Ibid.

265   Ibid.

266   D. T. Max, "Happiness 101," *New York Times*, January 7, 2007.

267   Ibid.

268   Ibid.

269   William J. Cromie, "How to Be Happy and Well Rather Than Sad and Sick," *Harvard University Gazette*, June 7, 2001, http://news.harvard.edu/gazette/legacy-gazette/#.

59. The Art of the Possible

270   Rosamund Stone Zander and Ben Zander, *The Art of Possibility: Transforming Professional and Personal Life* (New York: Penguin, 2000), 27.

271   Ibid.

272   Ibid., 33.

60. Popping Back

273   Robert Brooks and Sam Goldstein, *Raising Resilient Children: Fostering Strength, Hope, and Optimism in Your Child* (New York: McGraw-Hill, 2001), 1.

274   Ibid., 2.

275   Elizabeth Debold et al., "Cultivating Hardiness Zones for Adolescent Girls: A Reconceptualization of Resilience in Relationships with Caring Adults," in *Beyond Appearance: A New Look at Adolescent Girls*, ed. Norine G. Johnson, Michael C. Roberts, and Judith Worell (Washington, DC: American Psychological Association, 1999), 190.

276   Ibid., 190-191.

277   Ibid., 193.

278   Ibid., 196.

279   Deborah Blum, "Finding Strength: How to Overcome Anything," *Psychology Today*, May

1,1998, http://www.psychologytoday.com/articles/199805/finding-strength-how-overcome-anything?page=2.

61. The Pursuit of Happiness

280 John Perry Barlow, "The Pursuit of Emptiness: Why Americans Have Never Been a Happy Bunch," *Forbes*, December 3, 2001, http://www.forbes.com/asap/2001/1203/096.html.

281 Ibid.

282 Judy Mann, *The Difference: Growing Up Female in America* (New York: Warner Books, 1994), 262.

283 JoAnn Deak, *How Girls Thrive: An Essential Guide for Educators (and Parents)* (Washington, DC: National Association of Independent Schools, 1998), 56.

62. Sweet Corn and Tomatoes

284 Jane M. Healy, *Endangered Minds: Why Children Don't Think—and What We Can Do about It* (New York: Simon and Schuster, 1990), 25.

285 David Elkind, *The Hurried Child: Growing Up Too Fast Too Soon* (Reading, MA: Addison-Wesley, 1988), 118.

286 Ibid.

287 "About This I Believe," This I Believe, accessed August 5, 2011, http://thisibelieve.org/about/.

63. Rethinking Happily Ever After

288 "Dorothy Gaters Quotes" Famous Quotes, accessed August 5, 2011, http://www.1-famous-quotes.com/quote/5572.

289 Joanne Lipman, "The Mismeasure of Woman," *New York Times*, October 23, 2009.

290 Ibid

291 Ibid.

292 Charlene Li, *Open Leadership: How Social Technology Can Transform the Way You Lead* (San Francisco: Jossey-Bass, 2010), 239.

64. In Her Element

293 Ken Robinson, interview by Mike Huckabee, *Fox News,* Fox, January 31, 2009, http://www.youtube.com/watch?v=f9OoSHZbBHQ.

294 Ibid.

295 Ibid.

296 Ibid.

297 Ibid.

65. The Confidence to Be

298 Daniel McGinn, "Vote of Confidence," *Newsweek*, October 24, 2005, http://www.newsweek.com/2005/10/23/vote-of-confidence.html.

299 Carl Jung, *Memories, Dreams, Reflections* (New York: Vintage Books, 1965), 325.

300 McGinn, "Vote of Confidence."

66. Better to Forgive

301 Frederic Luskin, *Forgive for Good: A Proven Prescription for Health and Happiness* (New York: HarperCollins, 2002), vii-viii.

67. How Can I Help?

302 "Quotations by Author: Sir Winston Churchill," The Quotations Page, accessed August 5, 2011, http://www.quotationspage.com/quotes/Sir_Winston_Churchill/.

303 Tracy Gary and Melissa Kohner, *Inspired Philanthropy: Creating a Giving Plan: A Workbook* (San Francisco: Jossey-Bass, 1998), xiv.

304 Ibid.

68. Great Expectations

305 James M. Banner Jr. and Harold C. Cannon, *The Elements of Teaching* (New Haven: Yale

University Press, 1997), 39.

306   Ibid.

307   Ibid.

308   Ibid.

69. Oops, Sorry

309   Sharon Jayson, "Why Don't Men Say 'I'm Sorry'?," *USA Today*, September 28, 2010.

310   Ibid.

311   Rachel Rettner, "Sorry! Study Shows Why Women Apologize More," Women's Health, Msnbc, September 27, 2010, http://www.msnbc.msn.com/id/39384763/ns/health-behavior.

312   Deborah Tannen, *I Only Say This Because I Love You: How the Way We Talk Can Make or Break Family Relationships throughout Our Lives* (New York: Ballentine Books, 2002), 98.

313   Ibid.

314   Ibid.

315   Ibid.

316   Ibid., 99.

317   Ibid.

318   Ibid.

70. Staying Connected

319   Edward M. Hallowell, *Connect: 12 Vital Ties That Open Your Heart, Lengthen Your Life, and Deepen Your Soul* (New York: Pocket Books, 1999), 3.

320   Ibid., 7.

321   Karen Stabiner, *All Girls: Single-Sex Education and Why It Matters* (New York: Berkley, 2002), 107.

322   JoAnn Deak, *How Girls Thrive*, 16.

323   Carol Gilligan, *In a Different Voice: Psychological Theory and Women's Development* (Cambridge, MA: Harvard University Press, 1982), 59.

324   Ibid.

325   Deak, *How Girls Thrive*, 56.

326   Ibid.

71.Facing Up to Facebook

327   William Deresiewicz, "Faux-Friendship," *Chronicle of Higher Education*, December 6, 2009, http://chronicle.com/article/Faux-Friendship/49308/.

328   Ibid.

329   Ibid

330   Ibid.

331   Ibid.

332   Ibid.

72. A Community Together

333   Patricia Hersch, *A Tribe Apart: A Journey into the Heart of American Adolescence* (New York: Ballantine, 1998), 22.

334   Ibid., 21.

335   Ibid., 22.

336   Ibid.

337   Ibid., 23.

73. Making Cool Decisions

338   Jon Gertner, "The Futile Pursuit of Happiness," *New York Times Magazine*, September 7, 2003, http://www.nytimes.com/2003/09/07/magazine/the-futile-pursuit-of-happiness.html?scp=1&sq=futile%20pursuit%20of%20happiness&st=cse.

339   Ibid.

340　Richard Knox, "The Teen Brain: It's Just Not Grown Up Yet," *Morning Edition*, National Public Radio, March 1, 2010, http://www.npr.org/templates/story/story.php?storyId=124119468.

341　Ibid.

342　Ibid.

343　Ibid.

74. The More the Merrier

344　David Brooks, "The Crossroads Nation," *New York Times*, November 8, 2010.

345　Ibid.

76. Privilege with Cost

346　Stephen O'Connor, "A Different West Side Story," *New York Times Book Review*, March 8, 1998, http://www.nytimes.com/1998/03/08/books/a-different-west-side-story.html.

347　Ibid.

348　William Chafe, in *Proceedings: The Seventy-Seventh Annual Meeting, National Association of Principals of Schools for Girls*, March 2, 1998, 58.

349　Peggy McIntosh, "White Privilege: Unpacking the Invisible Knapsack" (1989), Resources Database, Learntoquestion, October 12, 2005, http://www.learntoquestion.com/resources/database/archives/000784.html.

77. Life Lessons

350　Robert J. Sternberg, e-mail message to author, July 8, 2011.

351　Ibid.

352　Ibid.

353　Portia Nelson, *There's a Hole in My Sidewalk: The Romance of Self-Discovery* (Hillsboro, OR: Beyond Words Publishing, 1993), 2. Copyright (c) 1993, by Portia Nelson, from the book *There's a Hole in My Sidewalk*. Reprinted with permission from Beyond Words Publishing, Hillsboro, Oregon.

78. Quality of Life

354　Andrew Revkin, "A New Measure of Well-Being from a Happy Little Kingdom," *New York Times*, October 4, 2005.

355　Ibid.

356　Ibid.

79. What Dreams Are Made Of

357　Renee Martin, "Women Entrepreneurs: Close the Gender Gap and Dream Big," *Forbes*, June 7, 2010, http://www.forbes.com/2010/06/07/small-business-loans-funding-forbes-woman-entrepreneurs-great-ideas.html.

358　Ibid.

359　Ibid.

360　Ibid.

About the Author

With thirty-three years of experience in independent education for girls, including sixteen years as the head of Miss Hall's School in Pittsfield, Massachusetts, Jeannie Norris is a respected leader and advocate in the area of all-girls education. She speaks and writes extensively about the education and parenting of girls, the role of women in philanthropy, and the effective management of independent schools. Norris grew up in Joplin, Missouri, where her parents raised her with the steadiness and confidence she espouses for today's parents. She and her husband, Peter, have between them four children and three grandchildren and make their home in North Carolina. **www.jeannienorris.com**